INVENTORY 98

To Raise, Destroy, and Create

For my mother

my wife

and my daughters

To Raise, Destroy, and Create:

The Poetry, Drama, and Fiction of
Imamu Amiri Baraka
(Le Roi Jones)

by

Henry C. Lacey

The Whitston Publishing Company
Troy, New York
1981

Library of Congress Catalog Card Number 80-50078

ISBN O-87875-185-8

Printed in the United States of America

ACKNOWLEDGMENTS

Corinth Books, Inc. Publishers. For excerpts from *Preface to a Twenty Volume Suicide Note*, by LeRoi Jones © 1961.

Dial Press. For excerpt from *Die Nigger Die!* by H. Rap Brown © 1969 by Lynne Brown.

The Drama Review. For excerpts from "Short Statement on Street Theatre" by Ed Bullins, *The Drama Review* v. 12, number 4, Summer 1968.

Macmillan Publishing Company. For excerpt from *Black Bourgeoisie*, by E. Franklin Frazier © 1962.

New Directions Publishing Corp. For excerpt from *Paterson*, by William Carlos Williams © 1948.

The New York Times Company. For excerpt from review of *El Hajj Malik*, by Clive Barnes © 1971.

Random House, Inc. For excerpts from *Invisible Man*, by Ralph Ellison © 1951.

The Sterling Lord Agency. For excerpts from *The Baptism* and *The Toilet* by LeRoi Jones (*The Baptism* © 1966 and *The Toilet* © 1963); *The Dead Lecturer*, by LeRoi Jones © 1964; *Four Black Revolutionary Plays*, by LeRoi Jones © 1969; *In Our Terribleness*, by LeRoi Jones © 1970; *Slave Ship*, by LeRoi Jones © 1967; *The System of Dante's Hell*, by LeRoi Jones © 1965.

Third World Press. For excerpt from *It's Nation Time*, by Imamu Amiri Baraka © 1970.

William Morrow and Company, Inc. For excerpt from *Crisis of*

PREFACE

Imamu Amiri Baraka first came to the attention of readers and critics in the late 1950's and early '60's under the name LeRoi Jones. At the outset of his career he published his poetry in various avant-garde literary journals, several of which he edited or co-edited, and was generally considered one of the more promising minor figures of the "Beat" movement. In his earliest works Baraka evinced not only the thematic concerns of Ginsberg, Kerouac, and Burroughs, but also the technical influences of such different poets as Yeats and Olson.

Almost from the beginning Baraka won the respect of serious critics, as in manifested in the favorable reviews of his first volume of poetry, *Preface to a Twenty Volume Suicide Note* (1961), and the acclaim accorded his early plays, *Dutchman* (1964) in particular. Denise Levertov's review of *Preface* is exemplary. In praise of the "sensuous and incantatory" beauty of the poems, Levertov says: ". . .in this first book, where the poems are arranged chronologically, one can see even as the chaff flies that the grain is good. His special gift is an emotive music that might have made him a 'lyric' poet, but his deeply felt preoccupation with more than personal issues enlarges the scope of his poems beyond what the term is often taken to mean."[1]

However, mainstream concern with Baraka as literary artist very nearly ceased in the latter half of the decade. Because of his growing militancy and increasingly energetic participation in the socio-political realm, Baraka's literary output, reflecting his new posture, was largely ignored. When treated at all, he was discussed as a revolutionary black nationalist peripherally concerned with "art." The following comment, taken from a review of *Home: Social Essays* (1966) is representative of the treatment given the latter works of Baraka. The reviewer says: "LeRoi Jones is still a young man, but it is now necessary to inter him as a writer, young and kicking. In his collection of essays from

1960-65, he writes and harangues himself out of the company of civilized men; and barring some surprising regeneration that is nowhere indicated, he forfeits all claim to serious attention, certainly as a social critic."[2]

This has too often been the attitude of critics regarding Baraka as social critic as well as artist. To clarify some of the confusion which even now obscures Baraka's significance, despite a number of recent ground-breaking studies, is one of my major aims. I hope to present the writer as artist at all stages of his development. Perhaps more so than any other writer, Baraka captures the idiom and style of modern urban black life. The uniqueness and authenticity of his work is largely attributable to his thorough knowledge of the speech and music of urban blacks. In his best work, he exploits these two powerful and rich possessions of an otherwise weak and impoverished people. He shows, especially in his later works, an understanding of the full range of black speech patterns, an element which invigorates and renders dramatic even his short stories and poems. Baraka's flawless ear retained also the sounds of modern jazz, the most important artistic creation of black America. Along with the frequent evidence of the traditional jazz framework, we see also in the poems the following characteristics of modern jazz: spontaneity of line, moving by sheer suggestiveness of impetus; eliptical phrasing; polyrhythmic thrust. Although similar musical qualities have been attributed to the work of other modern American poets, the conscious and effective employemnt of these qualities cannot be questioned in Baraka's case, for his musical insights are not only integrated into the artistic methods of his plays, poems, and stories. They have been articulated in a number of perceptive essays, as well as the extremely important study *Blues People.* Throughout his literary career, Baraka has been concerned greatly with the sounds of black life. During the latter 1960's and early 1970's, this concern took on even more importance in his attempts to reach a largely non-reading audience.

Baraka is among the most influential of black American writers because his example has been followed by younger black artists of every conceivable medium. In forsaking the closed circle of Village literati, Baraka turned to the creation of a more "functional" or socially committed art, an art concerned with shaping the minds of black Americans. His example inflamed the imaginations of many aspiring writers, musicians, and visual artists during the late '60's. We can trace Baraka's influence in the mature work of such black writers as Ed Bullins (drama), David Henderson (poetry), and Ishmael Reed (poetry and fiction), to name only a few. Although these and other Baraka-influenced writers have since eschewed the leader's extreme didacticism, Baraka was vital to their development in that he taught them to value their own experiences and to understand that they, too, had "access to a real world," one as open to artistic recreation as any other.

Not the least of Baraka's contributions to the younger writers is his demonstration, rather paradoxically, of the limitations of "protest" writing. Faced with Baraka's bitter but finely crafted studies of black-white conflict, conflict surpassing that of Wright or Baldwin, and presented in the most immediate genre, drama, the more talented disciples were forced to seek new directions. They began to deal, as does Baraka himself, more intensely with the intragroup experiences of blacks. Thus, in a very real sense, Baraka frees the younger writers to create instead of react.

A developmental study of the writings of Baraka is important, moreover, because the psychic turmoil of this particular atist reflects strongly the recent emotional history of collective black America. Following the feverish and disillusioning attempt to come to terms with white America during the last decade, black Americans suddenly realized that they had not come to terms with themselves. They learned that they were bound by a self-hatred more devastating than the hatred from racist whites could ever be. In his development Baraka presents a striking example of this painful longing for a positive sense of self. His spiritual journey, then, can and must be seen as a microcosmic presentation of the black American's crisis of identity, purpose, and direction, the crsis of the '60's. Baraka's major achievement lies in his artistic reordering of this crisis.

Although he has written perceptive social essays, important musical criticism, and an ever-increasing corpus of philosophical and political tracts, this study will be concerned primarily with the poetry, drama, and fiction produced by Baraka between the years 1960 and 1970. I have structured my consideration of the writer's progress in four chapters: Chapter I, "Schwartze Bohemian"; Chapter II, "Joseph to His Brothers"; Chapter III, "Imamu"; and Chapter IV, "Recapitulation."

Chapter I focuses on those works written during Baraka's "Beat" period. The bulk of this chapter consists of close analyses of the poems of *Preface to a Twenty Volume Suicide Note,* his first collected poems, and discussions of the early plays *The Baptism* and *The Toilet.* In these works the writer's concern with the racial theme is present but extremely muted in comparison with the later works. The poems, however, are marked by a pervasive sense of despair, alienation, and self-deprecation. At this point, Baraka shares the Beats' condemnation of the evils of convention, pretense, and "Moloch," Ginsberg's appellation for a materialistic and deathly America. The essentially non-racial plays are also concerned with these evils. The works of this period are further distinguished by a growing concern with the poetic process, as the writer reveals his distress over the questions of audience and commitment. These are the same concerns which dominate the works to be studied in the second chapter.

Chapter II, "Joseph to His Brothers," consists of in-depth analyses of the crucil transitional works of Baraka, those writings in which he begins to question his involvement in isolationist aesthetics and to reassess his existence as black man in America. The works to be treated here are the second major collection of poems, *The Dead Lecturer,* and two plays, *Dutchman,* and *The Slave.* The self-hatred of *Preface* is even more pronounced in these works. However, this anguish stems from the poet's sense of alienation from his black roots. Much of the writing of this period is addressed generally to the white reading public and specifically to the poet's literary peers. In attempting to break free of their influence, Baraka frequently chides himself and his former colleagues for their aesthetic distance. At the same time, he is groping for a rapport with black America and seeking to reconcile his emerging political stance with his art.

Chapter III, "Imamu," discusses the poet's rebirth (symbolized in the taking of a new name) as engaged black artist, concerned with what he comes to speak of as "consciousness raising." Works to be considered here are: *Black Magic Poetry, 1961-67,* a collection of three volumes of Baraka's verse; *Four Revolutionary Black Plays,* including *Experimental Death Unit #1, A Black Mass, Great Goodness of Life,* and *Madheart;* and the play *Slave Ship.* These works, addressed specifically to blacks, contain an abundance of African and Afro-American references. Special consideration will be given to the drama because of Baraka's heavy emphasis on drama as the most appropriate and effective means of reaching a largely unlettered audience. Moreover, the chapter will be concerned with some attempt to evaluate the artistic merits of these avowedly diadactic creations.

Chapter IV, "Recapitulation," focuses on the fiction written by Baraka. Works to be considered are *The System of Dante's Hell,* the author's only novel, and *Tales,* a collection of short stories and sketches. Primary consideration will be given to the analysis of *Tales,* which I feel is: (1) an extremely original contribution to short story writing; (2) paradoxical proof that Baraka was not entirely successful in ridding himself of early influences; (3) highly autobiographical; *i.e.,* it is, indeed, a "recapitulation" of the progression that is my central concern in this study.

I take this opportunity to express my deepest gratitude to Sheldon N. Grebstein for his many insights and constant encouragement during the writing of this work. Without his prompt and constructive critical assistance, this study would never have been completed. I would like also to acknowledge my indebtedness to Robert Kroetsch, Loften Mitchell and Bernard Rosenthal, who provided invaluable assistance during the early stages of my writing.

For assistance, critical and otherwise, during the latter stages of this work I wish to thank Tom Dent, members of the Dillard University English Department—Kenneth Brown, David Lambert and Helen Malin in particular. I extend special thanks to Monte Piliawsky for his commiseration and encouragement, to President Samuel DuBois Cook, Dr. Elton Harrison, and the Dillard University Administration for kindnesses extended during the final preparation of the manuscript, to my secretary, Sylvia Parks, and to Mr. and Mrs. Stephen Goode. There are so many others who gave inspiration and assistance in ways that they, perhaps, can not imagine. Here I would like to mention just a few such persons—Fred Foss, Joe Whittaker, Robert Bain, Miller Taylor, Dr. Edward E. Riley, Dr. Daniel C. Thompson, Horace Rice. I thank them all.

Finally, I extend a special thanks to my wife, Val, my daughters, Adrienne, Lynette, and Cecily, and my mother, Marguerite, all of whom sustained me and never stopped believing.

NOTES

[1]Denise Levertov, *Nation*, CXCIII, 12 (14 October 1961): 252.

[2]*Newsweek*, LXVII (2 May 1966): 106.

Chapter I

Die Schwartze Bohemien: *"The Terrible Disorder of a Young Man"*

Imamu Baraka, christened Everett LeRoi Jones, was born October 7, 1934, in Newark, New Jersey, the son of postal employee Coyt LeRoi Jones and social worker Anna Lois (Russ) Jones. (These parental occupations are referred to frequently in Baraka's transparently autobiographical writings.) *Current Biography*, 1970, notes that the writer exhibited his creative bent even as a pre-adolescent.[1] Deeply affected by the popular culture heroes of his youth, the young Baraka created his own comic strips and science fiction tales. We see the importance of these creations and the models from which they were drawn as late as *Preface* (1961) and *Tales* (1967). In the former the author attempts to rediscover the values posited by certain pop cult heroes. In the latter, the early interest in science fiction is reflected in a chilling tale of black humor called "Answers in Progress." Upon entering Newark's Barringer High School, Baraka was able to channel his energies through vigorous involvement with the school newspaper. He graduated from Barringer two years earlier than those in his age group.

After one year at the Newark branch of Rutgers University, Baraka enrolled at predominantly black Howard University, Washington, D. C. He briefly considered both religion and pre-medicine, but decided to major in English. Baraka graduated from Howard in 1953 with a major in English and a minor in philosophy. It was during his stay at Howard University, depicted as "the capstone of Negro education" (with pride or derision, depending on the source) by blacks, that Baraka observed the full scope of the pretensions of black middle class life. In an interview with the *San Francisco Chronicle*, the writer speaks of the effect of his years at Howard. He says "The Howard thing let me understand the Negro sickness. . . . They teach you how to pretend to be white."[2] Baraka left "the capstone" with an abundance of material which he used later in his recurring treatment of the theme of "false Negroes." For example, "The Alternative," a story from *Tales*, and one of his most thoroughgoing treatments of the self-delusions of the black bourgeoisie, takes place on a fictionalized version of the Howard campus.

Following his graduation from Howard, Baraka served in the United States Air Force. He served much of his tour at Ramsay Field, Puerto Rico, and left with a cynicism surpassing even that of his post-baccalaureate mood. In the same interview with the *San Francisco Chronicle*, he says of the Air Force, ". . . the Air Force made me understand the white sickness. It shocked me into realizing what was happening to me and others. By oppressing Negroes, the whites have become oppressors, twisted in the sense of doing bad things to people and justifying them finally, convincing themselves they are right, as people have always convinced themselves."[3] The Air Force experience forced another, more important revelation on him, however. It was during his Air Force years that Baraka began to think seriously of himself as a writer.

Partly in an attempt to ward off the ennui of the day-to-day regimentation of military life, he immersed himself in literature. Not only did he write—he read ravenously. Like the protagonist of the story "Salute," a story which draws heavily on the writer's Air Force experience, Baraka can say, "The Air Force was where I did all my reading, or a great deal of it. At least it was where I started coming on like a fullup intellectual and got silent and cagey with most of the troops and stayed in my room most nights piling through *Ulysses* or Eliot or something else like that."[4] One can, without exaggeration, compare his fervor to that of such figures as Malcolm X, Eldredge Cleaver, and Etheridge Knight. Like these writers, Baraka managed not only to survive an "incarceration," but to sustain himself through a fierce dedication to the written word.

Baraka studied comparative literature at Columbia University after his Air Force stint. It was during this period that he became involved with the so-called "Beat Generation," or the remnants of it. Along with his first wife, Hettie (Cohen) Jones, whom he married in 1958, Baraka edited *Yugen*, a journal dedicated to the presentation of the works of lesser-known East Village poets and others as well. During this period, *i.e.*, the later 1950's and early '60's, Baraka, along with Diane di Prima, co-edited an underground literary newsletter called *Floating Bear*. Also with Diane di Prima, he founded, in 1961, the American Theatre for Poets, an experimental dramatic troupe which read the works of various poets and dramatists in local coffee houses. Baraka had become such a central figure among the Village artists by 1964 that, without undue exaggeration, he rated feature treatment in an article entitled "King of the East Village."[5]

Theodore Hudson's *From LeRoi Jones to Amiri Baraka* (1973) presents a fairly detailed account of not only this period in the author's life, but the biography in general. His interview with the writer's former wife is especially useful with respect to the earliest works, works written while the writer was being lionized by critics and theatre-goers as both the heir apparent to James Baldwin and the dominant voice of the lower East Side. It was during this period that the home of "Roi" and Hettie served as a cultural center for avant-garde artists of all mediums. Writers, painters, and jazz musicians were frequent guests. In the midst of these energetic rebels, Baraka published his earliest poems and plays, works which show not only his kinship to the Beats, but works that also introduce those gnawing personal concerns that ultimately tear him from this coterie. The remainder of this chapter will be concerned with close analyses of works I consider most representative of Baraka's early "Village period." These works are *Preface to a Twenty Volume Suicide Note*, a collection of poems, and *The Baptism* and *The Toilet*, two early plays.

Preface (1961), though it appeared near the end of the Beat movement, is nonetheless representative of the Beat psyche. Clellon Holmes, in one of the first treatments of the Beat Generation, described the characteristic attitude in this way: "More than mere weariness, it implies the feeling of having been used, of being raw. It involves a sort of nakedness of mind and ultimately of soul; a feeling of being reduced to the bedrock of consciousness. In short, it means being undramatically pushed up against the wall of oneself."[6] It is this feeling that dominates the poems of *Preface*. In these lyrical outpourings of a thoroughly drained soul, we find the ultimate pessimism. Even love, the sole sustaining factor for the earlier, more optimistic Beats, is an inverted or "evol" thing in these poems. The gospel of love is preached only in his plays of this period, which will be discussed later in this chapter.

The poems of this first collection, characterized by a pervasive sense of despair, alienation, and self-deprecation, reflect also the Beats' scorn for the pressures exerted by the forces of convention pretense, and materialism. The classic Beat response to these forces, however, was one of cool disengagement. One recognized ugliness, perhaps wrote poems about it, but one did not become so "uncool" as to think he could actually *do* anything about it. Much of the tension in the poems of *Preface* stems from this young black Beat poet's struggle to replace his cool withdrawal with a sense of commitment. The degree of his discomfort with disengagement reaches its peak, of course, in his dramatic break with the Village scene some four years later. This early questioning of the merits of cool disengagement must, undoubtedly, be seen in light of the times. Baraka, though often cynical in his comments on the Civil Rights Movement of the early '60's, was profoundly affected by it. His awareness of the new black activism, coupled with a first hand, almost apocalyptic, experience in post revolution Cuba, all but destroyed his cool indifference. The evidence of the struggle lies in the poems.

Like the writings of the earlier Beats, the poems of *Preface* attack the distorted values of a commercially oriented society. Though it is seldom as explicitly articulated, as in, say, *Howl*, this theme is implied throughout the collection. It is most evident in the despairing and self-deprecating lyrics that grow out of the poet's conviction that he is not capable of countering the forces of evil with a spiritualizing force. Along with these central concerns, the poet includes the theme of racial identity. Baraka's early technique, which will be given more extensive treatment later, is characterized by eliptical phrasing and spontaneity of movement, both of which have led some critics to compare his poems to jazz music.

In the title poem of *Preface*, the reader immediately discerns the voice of "the American existential," Norman Mailer's term for the possessor of the Beat attitude. The speaker of "Preface to a Twenty Volume Suicide Note" is indeed

> . . . the man who knows that if our collective condition is to live with instant death by atomic war, relatively quick death by the State as *l'universe concentrationnaire*, or with a slow death by conformity with every creative and rebellious instinct stifled . . . why then the only life-giving answer is to accept the terms of death, to live with death as immediate danger, to divorce oneself from society, to exist without roots, to set out on that uncharted journey to the rebellious imperatives of the self.[7]

Given his understanding of himself and of his world, this is the lure, the compelling attraction from which the poet must divorce himself. In the title poem, the speaker accepts the threatening nature of the

modern world. It is a world in which he, the time-bound urban dweller, is prepared to meet lurking death on every street corner.

> Lately, I've become accustomed to the way
> The ground opens up and envelopes me
> Each time I go out and walk the dog.
> Or the broad edged silly music the wind
> Makes when I run for a bus. . .

The poet as hipster feels profoundly the pressures of the "straight
life," the life of convention and respectability, in this introductory
poem. There is the recurring impatience with those forces that bind
him to schedules. Enthralled by the powers of a competitive, materialistically oriented society, he is left with one refuge, the imagination. It has even become impossible to transcend his ugly surround-
ings in this manner, however. Limitations have been placed on the
poet's most compelling images of transcendence and wonder. Having
become finite, the stars no longer inspire visionary experiences. The
final six lines of this introductory poem deepen the despair.

> And then last night, I tiptoed up
> To my daughter's room and heard her
> Talking to someone, and when I opened
> The door, there was no one there. . .
> Only she on her knees, peeking into
> Her own clasped hands.

That the idea of God does not enter the speaker's mind is some indication of the degree of his disillusionment, a disillusionment made
more poignant by contrasting it to the idealism of the child.

The poem achieves much of its effect through the employment
of certain structural and aural devices. First, the poem employs a
logical, sequential movement, the three major stazas beginning "Late-
ly," "And now," "And then." There is, moreover, an effective down,
up, down progression in the visual imagery of the three stanzas. Finally, the concluding lines play a number of variations on the mourn-
ful "o" sound ("tiptoed," "room," "opened," "door," "no one,"
"only," "own") with profoundly appropriate effect.

"Way Out West (for Gary Snyder)," like "Preface," reflects

the poet's sense of the despair that is an essential part of each waking day in the city.

> As simple an act
> as opening the eyes
> *[. . . .]
> Morning: some tear is broken
> on the wooden stairs
> of my lady's eyes. Profusions
> of green. The leaves. Their
> constant prehensions. Like old
> junkies on Sheridan Square, eyes
> cold and round. There is a song
> Nat Cole sings . . . This city
> & the intricate disorder
> of the seasons

In the Daliesque image of his "lady's" pain, we get one of the many recurring images of the failure of love and the difficulty of maintaining an equilibrium in domestic affairs, for in this collection the family life of the poet frequently symbolizes the implacable pull of convention. The landscape, "Profusions/of green. The leaves," only serves to mock his decadence. The seasons are "disordered" because they do not perpetually reflect the wintry nature of his inner being. The poet also broods about the passage of time and his loss of innocence.

> I am distressed. Thinking
> of the seasons, how they pass,
> how I pass, my very youth, the
> ripe sweet of my life; drained off . . .

The lament for the bygone days of adolescence recurs frequently in the confessional of the hipster. It is a central concern in the extremely personal poems of *Preface*. Though primarily concerned with the immediacy of his situation, the speaker of these poems cannot completely reject the symbolic weight of his youthful days. Gene Feldman explains the meaning of adolescence in the Beat

---

* [. . .] ellipses mine, indicating omission of words or lines. Hereafter shown in brackets without notation.

mentality in the following manner: "In stepping out of the competitive area which custom has marked as the proving ground of manhood, [the Beatnik] is forced back into the marginal existence of the
adolescent."[8] The days of adolescence bring not only memories of
freedom from the stifling pressures of adult convention. They also
project images of certitude and the possibility of belief, the central
concerns in such poems as "In Memory of Radio" and "Look for
You Yesterday, Here You Come Today," both of which will be discussed later.

The speaker of "Way Out West" is too preoccupied with the
malaise of the moment to dwell on the meaning of his adolescence.
He knows too well the pain of taking on the prophetic role in a soul-
less society. Hence his identification with the unheeded, impotent
seer, Tiresias. With this grim realization of his inadequacy, the poet
turns to the comtemplation of suicide, another dominant theme of
the poems. He imagines himself ending his life by drowning.   The
last two lines of the poem balance the first two, bringing the poem
full circle. Beginning with the death-in-life of another waking day in
the city, the poem ends with the projection of release through the
actuality of death.

"The Bridge (# for Wieners and McClure)" is a masterful rendering of the themes of the poems just discussed. Here, however, the
ideas are couched in the jargon of the jazz musician, a sacred figure
with the Beats. Although in his article, "The Pre-Revolutionary Writings of Imamu Amiri Baraka,"[9] William C. Fischer shows remarkable appreciation of the musical underpinning of this poem, his insistence on seeing it simply as a "sharp message" of rejection to his
fellow poets is too narrow a reading. More than merely a rejection of
the poetic art and values of Wieners and McClure, "The Bridge" is
the anguished cry of a man who has lost control of his life. Symbolically, however, he is a musician who has lost control in the middle
of an improvisation.

> I have forgotten the head
> of where I am. Here at the bridge. 2
> bars, down the street, seeming
> to wrap themselves around my fingers, the day,
> screams in me; pitiful like a little girl

you sense will be dead before the winter
is over.

In jazz parlance, the "head" is the theme or written portion of a
musical composition. It is that part of a selection that opens and
closes the traditional jazz rendition. The improvisation, or "blowing"
section, is always framed by the "head." The "bridge," while a part
of the "head" or theme, is that part of the theme that the layman
calls the chorus. As Fischer points out, the bridge, because it is repeated fewer times, is the most difficult passage for the working
musician to remember. Having forgotten the "head," *i.e.*, his purpose, the speaker of "The Bridge" has been thrust, in the midst of his
improvisation, *i.e.*, life, into the most difficult section of his performance. The poem, in spite of its intensity, is not without humor.
This is evident in the use of the *double entendre*. The "bars" are, on
the one hand, saloons in which the speaker hopes to drown his despair. They are, on the other hand, musical measures, representing
the point of his progress through this, the most crucial moment of
his performance, *i.e.*, existence. The image of the incapacitated fing-
ers reinforces the portrait of the speaker as musician, deprived of his
erstwhile ability to articulate his musical ideas.

In the second stanza, the speaker asks, "How does the bridge
go?" Fischer correctly notes that this is " . . . the question every
working musician has asked a hundred times."[10] This question
focuses sharply on the plight of the persona/musician whose life is an
improvisation gone awry. His situation is given clarity in the following lines:

[. . .] The changes are difficult when
you hear them & know they are all in you, the chords
of your disorder meddle with your would be disguises.

Having forgotten the "changes" (chord progressions), the player produces only dissonant effects, reflective of the chaos of his personal
life. It is at this point that the *double entendre* is invoked again, but
this time in a markedly more tragic manner. The "bridge" becomes
quite literally the span from which the speaker leaps in suicide. As in
"Way Out West," the speaker ends with a projected sucidal release.

Although this work, in its articualtion of urban despair and its

extensive employment of musical metaphors, calls to mind Hart
Crane's epic poem of the same title, it is more closely related to the
very music which supplied its symbols. To those familiar with jazz
music of the late '50's and early '60's, this poem brings to mind tenor
saxophone giant Sonny Rollins, who at a crucial point in his career
withdrew from society to contemplate and perfect his art. He frequently practiced alone, atop the Williamsburg Bridge. This period in
Rollins' development has since come to be known as Rollins' "bridge
period." Baraka, always a student and leading critic of the music, was
surely aware of the now ledgendary decision of Rollins. The result of
this awareness is "The Bridge," wherein the musician's anguish is
merged with that of the poet. This connection becomes even more
plausible when we consider the title of the poem preceding "The
Bridge" in *Preface*. It is "Way Out West." Rollins recorded an album
bearing this title. Baraka's high regard for this musicians's artistry is
seen again in his review of Rollins' album "What's New," published
in 1963. In this review Baraka goes so far as to say, "Rollins is one of
the marvels of our grim little age, and it pains me to think of men
talking knowledgeably about what is of value in the world without
their having heard him."[11] Rollins is symbol for the soul in guest of
order, and as such he is important to the poet of *Preface,* who shares
his ideal.

   The suicidal urge is a recurrent motif is several of the poems of
Preface. Utterly bored, impatient with a world devoid of humanizing
values, and tormented by the feeling that he can effect no change in
such a world, the poet is frequently obsessed with the idea that
actual death will release him from what amounts to a death in life.
This is most evident in the poems just discussed. Those poems that
do not end in death-hauntedness evince extreme self-loathing. "The
Turncoat" is typical:

> [. . .] I am alone & brooding, locked in
> with dull memories & self hate, the terrible disorder
> of a young man.

In "Vice" he speaks scathingly of his disengagement:

> [. . .] All the things I can talk about
> mean nothing to me
> This is *not* rage. (I am not that beautiful!) Only

immobile coughs & gestures towards somethings I don't
understand. If I were lucky enough to still be an
adolescent, I'd just slink off merrily to masturbate.
Mosaic of disorder I own but cannot recognize. Mist
in me.

The word "disorder," conspicuously present in "Way Out West" and "The Bridge," is invoked once again. It is easily the most frequently recurring word in the collection. Each use of this word underscores the spiritual torpor of the persona as he fumbles for release from ennui and purposelessness. *Preface* must be read as a desperate attempt on the part of the poet to impose some order on his personal life and that of the world in general. Constantly aware of the debilitating influence of his milieu, *i.e.*, the Beat culture, he repeatedly flagellates himself for not fully exercising his prophetic powers and actually working toward the establishment of a new moral order. The path Baraka was to take in directing his own moral energies is especially evident in the poems inspired by his Cuban experience. Those works, "One Night Stand" and "Betancourt," will be discussed later. Before the poet is able to take on the new posture dictated by his Cuban experience, however, he can only look back to his adolescent days to vestiges of order and humanistic values. True heroism and virtuous action are exhibited only in the worlds of radio drama and comic strips.

Those few critics who have dealt with the poems of *Preface* have noted Baraka's concern with the popular culture myths of his adolescent years. The critics, however, have often misread the meaning of this pervasive element in the poems. William Fischer's statements are typical of those who too vigorously seek evidence of the embryonic *Baraka* in the early poems of *Jones*. In his otherwise perceptive essay, Fischer sees the poet rejecting the heroes of movie and comic book simply as expressions of the angry black poet's "acrid satire on various aspects of American culture during the years of World War II and after. . . ."[12] Other commentators have reached similar conclusions, seeing the popular culture heroes as merely destructive images, images justifying a long history of racial injustice and evil.

Denise Levertov, however, as early as 1961, in her review of *Preface*, comes much closer to the real meaning of the popular culture images in the poems. Levertov says that Baraka had the "kind of childhood in which the old comic strips—Moon Mullins, Krazy Kat, *etc.*,—gave to the imagination, for which no other place was provided, a space in which to grow. Jazz, too, has been for [the poet and his contemporaries], and remains (one can hear it is the movement of [his] lines) a taken-for-granted and essential part of the world, an air to breathe when otherwise they would have stifled."[13] Levertov's comment, moreover, shows an understanding of the meaning of popular myth to the Beats in general (Jack Kerouac, when asked to define the Beat Generation, once said, "Being Beat goes back to my ancestors, to the rebellious, the weird, the mad. To Laurel and Hardy, to Popeye, to Lamont Cranston, the Shadow, with his insane heh-heh-heh laugh. . . .").[14] Another commentator, Lee A. Jacobus, in his article "Imamu Amiri Baraka: The Quest for Moral Order," shows even fuller understanding of those figures as they appear in the poems. Jacobus says: "Throughout the early work, Jones constantly links his comic book heroes with the search for moral order. Those heroes are not only men of action, but men of understanding. . . ."[15] A careful reading of such works as the frequently anthologized "In Memory of Radio," "Look for You Yesterday, Here You Come Today," "The Death of Nick Charles," and "Duke Mantee" gives irrefutable support to Jacobus's statement. The figures treated in these works symbolize the certitude and righteous commitment the bored poet finds so lacking his own life.

In the opening lines of "In Memory of Radio," Baraka refers specifically to Jack Kerouac's noted reverence for Lamont Cranston, also known as "the Shadow," popular character from the days of radio drama.

> Who has ever stopped to think of the divinity of Lamont Cranston?
> (Only Jack Kerouac, that I know of: & Me.
> The rest of you probably had on WCBS and Kate Smith,
> Or something equally unattractive.)

The sanctity of Cranston, in these extremely "campy" lines, is opposed to the implied spiritual failure of Kate Smith, who made a career of singing "God Bless America." In the eyes of the poet, her life is dedicated to the perpetuation of a blind super-patriotism or, at least, a moral laxity which approves even the most destructive powers of "Moloch." Along with Kate Smith, he recalls other radio and early television personalities. Perhaps it is important that these figures are primarily remembered for their efforts in television, the medium that brought the end to the completely imaginative response elicited by radio.

> [. . .] I do not have the healing powers of Oral Roberts . . .
> I cannot, like F. J. Sheen, tell you how to get saved & *rich!*

The failure of these two figures is two-fold. By confusing the spiritual and the material and by encouraging false hope, they have abused the holy, imaginative medium of radio. They have also profaned the priesthood. If these are our spiritual leaders, it is no wonder, then, that in such a society all human values have been inverted.

> [. . .] Love is an evil word.
> Turn it backward/see, see what I mean?
> An evol word.

Baraka asserts that we can overcome this perversion only through immersion in the sacred realm of the imagination, the spirit. This was possible with radio and the liberating powers of such programs as "Red Lantern" and "Let's Pretend." These concluding lines convince us of the rightness of Levertov's explanation. The poem ends by returning to the point of departure. Again we are reminded of "the divinity of Lamont Cranston," a supernaturally gifted force for goodness and law in a spiritually impoverished world.

> What was it he used to say (after the transformation, when he was
> safe
> & invisible & the unbelievers couldn't throw stones?) "Heh, heh,
> heh,
> Who knows what evil lurks in the hearts of men? The Shadow
> knows."
> O, yes he does
> O, yes he does.
> An evil word it is,
> This Love.

In "Look for You Yesterday, Here You Come Today" the poet reiterates all the themes seen in the preceding poems. Like "The Bridge," the poem is partially rooted in Afro-American musical expression. The title of this poem is also that of a classic Jimmy Rushing blues tune. The speaker evinces the alienation, self-hate, the death-hauntedness of the previously discussed poems. This poem is most closely related, however, to those works positing the certitude available to the young aficionado of popular myth, *i.e.*, the "Believer." Once more we witness the anguish of another waking day in the city.

> Morning never aids me in my quest.
> I have to trim my beard in solitude.
> I try to hum lines from "The poet in New York."

The allusion to Lorca is most interesting when considered in light of the poem "Hymn for Lanie Poo," to be discussed later. The influence of the Spanish poet is profoundly felt in this particular work. Here, however, art and the proper concerns of poetry are, by implication, thematic issues. This becomes especially evident with the utterances of the jaded editor of the "little magazine."

As in the poem "Vice," Baraka also excoriates himself for the absence of "rage" or engagement. The implied image of the poet as cowboy not only prepares us for the later entrance of the Lone Ranger, but also indicates the path that Baraka wants his writings to take. Like the unspecified "Great Poets" referred to in this poem, he wants, literally, to fight with words. As yet, however, he has found no belief capable of releasing him from his deathly, Beat, *i.e.*, "defeated," withdrawal. Once upon a time he was able to respond to the world with a romantic readiness. But, like all "the best minds of [his] generation," he had the misfortune

> To arise one smoking spring
> & find one's youth has taken off
> [...]
> & all my piddling joys retreated
> to their dopey mythic worlds.

Continuing to speak in this extremely explicit manner, a manner not at all typical of these early poems, the poet laments that "There is probably no such place as Battle Creek, Michigan?" The sardonic humor of this line sets the tone for the remainder of the poem. As in

"In Memory of Radio," the poet juxtaposes the very real weight of his despair with the "dopey mythic worlds" of his youth. The result is a tragicomic effect akin to that elicited by the blues. With this in mind, we see that the poet did not haphazardly choose the title of this poem. The poet, like the bluesman, laughs to keep from crying.

No longer able to believe in the existence of the box-top redemption center of the universe, the disenchanted speaker of "Look for You Yesterday . . ." comes to the conclusion that the innocence of his adolescent days will no longer suffice. This is made obvious in his appropriation of the blues lyric that gives the poem its title as well as its sense of irretrievable loss:

> 'Look for you yesterday
> Here you come today
> Your mouth wide open
> But what you got to say?'

The lyric ends with a final reference to the disarmed poet, the poet incapable of moral action or "a simple straightforward anger." His loss of belief is imaged again with references to the more identifiable accoutrements of the comic book hero. The pervasive blues tone, concretely establishing the sense of loss, is reeemphasized in the final lines. In this manner the tragic and comic are finally, and most effectively, yoked:

> My silver bullets all gone
> My black mask trampled in the dust
>
> & Tonto way off in the hills
> Moaning like Bessie Smith.

Like Lamont Cranston, Nick Charles, Dashiel Hammett's cool detective, is a figure of purpose and moral direction. In the poem "The Death of Nick Charles," the poet, through the implication of the title, equates the death of love with the invalidation of belief in Nick Charles' heroism. There is no explicit reference to Charles in the poem. The poem is concerned with a dying or dead love affair. Just as the poet equated Lamont Cranston with the now lost imaginative response, he equated the hero of "The Thin Man" radio series with love. He refers to the failure of this particular love affair with images

from music and the dance. Much like the speaker of the title poem of
Preface, the speaker of this poem equates loss of love to the absence
of music. His lament, "Nobody sings anymore," is identical to the
concern of this particular poem. The poet realizes, moreover, that his
self-deprecating and death-haunted poetry will in no way serve as
music. It will not facilitate the dance of consummation. In Prufrock-
ian manner, he says:

> [. . .] (and this is not
> what I mean. Not the thing I wanted for you. Not, finally.
> *Music*, only terror at this lightly scribbled day.

The grating and insufficient sounds of "words" come also from the
loved one. Addressing her, the speaker says:

> Something
> like loathing
> covers your words.
> [. . .]
> And these words
> are not music. They make no motions
> for a dance.

The world of these lovers is one in which consummation, as symbolized by the dance, is no longer possible. There are, however, exceptions to this sterile confrontation in other poems of this collection.
The most notable of these are the two warm but ironical poems dedicated to Hettie, the poet's first wife, and the lyrical poem entitled
"The Clearing." The Edenic, dream-like meeting experienced by the
lovers of "The Clearing" is sharply undercut, nevertheless, by the
aridity of "The Death of Nick Charles," which immediately follows
the former poem in the collection.

In sharp contrast to the poems discussed to this point are
"One Night Stand" and "Betancourt," both of which grew out of the
poet's visit to Cuba in 1960. Baraka, along with several other black
intellectuals, was invited to Cuba to take part in a celebration of the
revolution and to see what was "actually happening" (to use Baraka's
words) in Cuba. This trip, described fully in "Cuba Libre," the first
essay in the collection *Home: Social Essay* (1966), is important to
the later development of Baraka's art. Cynical, distrusting absolutist

programs of the left or the right, Baraka evidently shared the sentiments of fellow poet Allen Ginsberg at the outset of the trip. Ginsberg's sentiments, originally taken from a letter written from Greece
on October 16, 1961, and published in *PA'LANTE* magazine in
1962, were later published as *Prose Contribution to Cuban Revolution* (1966). Ginsberg Says:

> All governments including the Cuban are still operating with the rules
> of identity forced on them by already outmoded modes of conscious-
> ness. I say outmoded since it has brought all Govts. to the edge of
> world destruction. No govt., not even the most Marxian revolutionary &
> well-intended like Cuba presumably, is guiltless in the general world
> mess, no one can afford to be righteous any more. Righteousness and
> right & wrong are still fakes of the old suicidal identity.[16]

Ginsberg goes on to surmise that because no innovative poetry
is coming out of Cuba, the censors of language are becoming more
powerful, an occurrence which leads to the ultimate evil, the "cen-
sorship of consciousness," a practice he felt more and more prevalent
in both America and Russia. He ends his comment with even stronger
reservations on the Cuban revolution. This poet's statement must
stand as a reliable approximation of Baraka's own attitude prior to
his Cuban visit. First, the essay "Cuba Libre" tells us as much. Second, the poem "One Night Stand" bears the dedicatory inscription
"for Allen."

"One Night Stand" open with major emphasis on the sounds
of new life:

> We entered the city at noon! High bells, the radio on
> Some kind of Prokofieff; snaring the violent remains of
> the day in sharp webs of dissonance.

The bells, the radio, and, particularly, the dissonant sounds of
Prokofieff all destroy the old harmonies. In the second stanza, there
are more images of the erosion of an older way of life. This time the
images are visual ("old gates", "iron doors . . . all grey," "Bricks
mossed over"). The third stanza, which combines auditory and visual
images, is concerned with apocalyptic images suggesting the destruction or purgation that must occur before the new order can be built.

It is not until the fifth stanza that we see direct reference to the
poet's attitude toward the new regime. He says:

> We come in, with our incredulousness, from the north.
> On steely highways from the marble entrails of noon.
> We had olives, and the green buds locked our lutes.

Though bearing the symbols of victory, peace, and plenitude, the
north-americano is not yet able to believe in the rightness of the
"well-intended" (to use Ginsberg's phrase) Cuban action. The poem
ends with the troubled American poet's perspective on his relationship, as black man, to the Cubans, particularly the black Cubans.
(In the sixth stanza, the poet refers to the impact of the revolution
on "loud black bondservants, dazed and out of their wool heads.")
The poet, in "One Night Stand," seeks the answers to two questions
that will plague him for some time. (1) Is it possible to regain a long
dead idealism, to act and effect change in the world? (2) What is his
relationship to black people and the third world in general? There is
no better explanation of the poet's attitude at this phase of his development than that found in the final stanza of "One Night Stand."
Referring to himself and his fellow black visitors, he says:

> We *are* foreign seeming persons. Hats flopped so the sun
> can't scald our beards; odd shoes, bags of books & chicken
> We have come a long way, & are uncertain which of the masks
> is cool.

Not only does he accept his alienation from those "loud black bondservants." The poet, in the best Beat manner, wants to know what
behavior (American or Afro-American?) "is cool," the ultimate term
for the disengaged Beatnik. By ending the poem with this very
weighty term, he shows us that, though shaken, his attitude toward
the Cuban action and its ramifications is at best ambiguous.

"Betancourt," like "One Night Stand," comes from the poet's
Cuban experience. This longer poem is even more important in
assessing the writer's evolving position. We see an indication of the
extreme significance of this poem in its dating, "30 July, 1960,
Habana." No other poem in the collection bears such a temporal
designation. The poet, for the first time, sees a way out of his paralysis. In Cuba, various young South American writers and intellectuals,

also guests at the celebration, convince the norteamericano that poets, too, can act decisively. "Betancourt" is dedicated to one of these influences, Senora Betancourt, described in "Cuba Libre" as "very short, very blonde and very pretty. . . . a Mexican delegate of the Youth Congress, a graduate student in economics at one of the universities, the wife of an economist, and a mother."[17] Baraka and the economist discussed at some length the ugliness and irrationality of life in the United States. Following one of the Senora's more spirited attacks on Americans, the poet included, Baraka is forced into his cool disengaged enclave. He says:

> I tried to defend myself, 'Look, why jump on me? I understand what you're saying. I'm in complete agreement with you. I'm a poet . . . what can I do? I write, that's all, I'm not even interested in politics.' She jumped on me with both feet as did a group of Mexican poets later in Habana. She called me a 'cowardly bourgeois individualist.' The poets, or at least one young wild-eyed Mexican poet, Jaime Shelley, almost left me in tears, stomping his foot on the floor, screaming: 'You want to cultivate your soul? In that ugliness you live in, you want to cultivate your soul? Well, we've got millions of starving people to feed, and that moves me enough to make poems out of.'[18]

Though it takes American poet LeRoi Jones several years to completely absorb the messages of Senora Betancourt and Jaime Shelley, absorb it he does, and the final result is the birth of Imamu Amiri Baraka.

The poem "Betancourt" is a poem of appreciation. Bearing the dedicatory inscription "for Rubi," it begins appropriately:

> What are
> influences?

He goes on to speak specifically of the Senora's assault on his deathly Americanness and is, furthermore, stunned at the irony of this tutorial relationship. It is indeed strange that the Western girl has embraced an essentially non-Western life style, while the transplanted African, with perhaps more cause for "radical" thought and action, has embraced Westernism completely. This paradox is specifically mentioned in one of several passages which make this poem, among other things, literally a love lyric.

> And last night, talking to overselves, except
> when some wildness
> cut us, ripped impossibly
> deep beneath black
> flesh
> to black bone. Then
> we loved each other. Understood
> the miles of dead air
> between our
> softest parts. French girl
> from the desert. Desert man,
> whose mind is some rotting
> country of snow.

The poet concludes with the understanding that the ordering he has so ardently desired can perhaps be found through the right uses of his art. Although not ready to become the fully committed, *i.e.* political, writer at this point, he has been sufficiently moved to change his definition of the word "poem".

> [. . .] (I think
> I know now
> what a poem
> is) a
> turning away . . .
> from what
> it was
> had moved
> us . . .

A poem, then, is not merely the instrument of change. It is change itself, the very principle of revolution. We see in the latter works of Baraka a crystalization of this attitude.

    Although we can see in this experience the seed of the poet's later rejection of Western esthetic principles altogether, at this juncture he seems to be concerned more with shaking the particular influence of the Village coterie than with taking on the Western fine arts tradition. This is made obvious by various comments in the essay

"Cuba Libre." The Poet senses that his intellectual friends, behind the fashionable facade of "proper knowing cynicism," are in actuality on the same wave length as the most reactionary forces of the times. He comes to the conclusion that the Beats' "so-called rebellion against what is most crass and ugly in our society . . ." is " . . . without the slightest thought of, say, any kind of direction or purpose."[19] Direction and purpose, we recall, are the two most desired elements in the brooding lyrics previously discussed. The final condemnation of himself and his friends reads: "The rebels among us have become merely people like myself who grow beards and will not participate in politics."[20]

Before leaving *Preface*, we must concern ourselves with yet another important matter, the racial theme. The most obvious difference between this first volume and Baraka's later work is seen in the young poet's sparing employment of the racial theme. In the latter works, every poem, story, play, or essay is in some way a statement on race. Though subtly evoked in some of the previously discussed poems, overt treatment of the theme is seen in only three of the poems of *Preface*. These poems are "One Night Stand", "Hymn for Lanie Poo," and "Notes for a Speech."

"Hymn for Lanie Poo," evidently addressed to the poet's sister Elaine, is the longest poem in the collection. The epigraph from Rimbaud—*Vous etes de faux Negres*—establishes the theme. In this poem we are given several damning images of assimilationist blacks, *i.e.* blacks who, in their own way, are as driven by a death wish as was our brooding poet. The primary example of this malaise is seen in the poet's sister, of whom he openly speaks in the final section of this seven-part poem. Once we realize that the poem is dedicated to the sister so scathingly denounced in the final section of the poem, we can safely assume that the "young black beautiful woman" of the first lines of the poem is indeed the same person. The poem begins:

O,
these wild trees
will make charming wicker baskets,
the young woman
the young black woman
the young black beautiful woman

said.
> These wild-assed trees
> will make charming
> wicker baskets.
> (now I'm putting words in her mouth . . . tch)

Throughout the poem we see the poetic imagination transforming the city in this manner. In the poem's opening lines, the speaker and his sister are in some imaginary primitive setting. The scene opens with the sister's "proper" remark on the idyllic scene. The speaker then attributes a more earthy or "hip" response to the sister but quickly rejects it as a possibility for her. This "young black beautiful woman," so wrapped up in hatred of things black, most assuredly hates the vitality of the black street idiom. In the first section of the poem, still in the imaginative setting, the poet hears the following warning, presumably from his sister:

> Beware the evil sun . . .
> turn you black
> turn your hair
> crawl your eyeballs
> rot your teeth.

The warnings, however, mean nothing to the speaker of the poem. He says:

> The God I pray to
> got black boobies
> got steatopygia

While the young woman spurns her blackness, the speaker embraces his with a religious fervor. The sister receives more condemnation in the description of her "coming out" party.:

> She had her coming out party
> with 3000 guests
> from all parts of the country.
> Queens, Richmond, Togoland, The Cameroons;
> A white hunter, very unkempt,
> with long hair,
> whizzed in on the end of a vine
> (spoke perfect english too.)

[. . .]
John Coltrane arrived with an Egyptian lady.
he played very well.
[. . .]
We got so drunk (Hulan Jack
brought his bottle of Thunderbird),
nobody went hunting
the next morning.

The black debutante's ball is one of the most frequently satir-
ized affairs in literature written by black Americans. One of the more
scathing treatments of this phenomenon is seen in John Killens'
novel *Cotillion*. The roots of this particular treatment of the debutante's ball and other such events are found in E. Franklin Frazier's
significant study, *Black Bourgeoisie* (1957), an attack on the emptiness and pretense of the so-called black middle class in America
(Acknowledging his debt to Frazier, who taught, until his death in
1962, at Howard University, Baraka entitled a later poem "Letter to
E. Franklin Frazier." This poem is included in *Sabotage*, which will
be briefly considered in chapter two.). This particular coming out
party is surely of the ostentatious variety so abhorred by the influential sociologist. The unnecessarily long guest list and the exotic
melange of types are all meant to *impress.*

As before, the poet uses elements from popular culture for
humorous effect. This affair is as much a production as a "Tarzan"
or "Jungle Jim" movie. Even the John Coltrane recording, probably
the classic ballad "Naima" (Egyptian lady), is used simply for its
appropriateness as mood music. This is surely, for Baraka, the ultimate blasphemy. The earlier praise of Sonny Rollins is mild in comparison to some of the things the writer has said about Coltrane.
Hulan Jack objectively epitomizes the theme of *faux Negres.* Jack,
former president of the Borough of Manhattan, and a prime example
of the black bourgeoisie, surely should have known that his station
behooved him to drink perhaps, scotch, not Thunderbird Wine, the
favorite drink of ghetto inhabitants during the '50's and early '60's.
The sixty-cent wine was so popular that the following lines were frequently used as a form of greeting among street people, even children:

What's the word?
Thunderbird!
What's the price?
Thirty twice!
Where ya' go?
Liquor sto'!

In the poem's terms, Hulan Jack makes the unforgivable slip in bringing his bottle of Thunderbird. But in doing so, he acknowledges his
roots, his kinship with even the lowest dregs of the black ghetto.
They, literally, share a common taste, but Jack, *faux Negre* that he
is, is driven to deny it. Ralph Ellison's protagonist in *Invisible Man*
goes to the heart of the matter when he suddenly realizes the sickness of the assimilationist dream and cultural shame. He says, "What
a group of people we were, I thought. Why you could cause us the
greatest humiliation simply by confronting us with something we
liked. Not *all* of us, but so many. Simply by walking up and shaking
a set of chitterlings or a well-boiled hog maw at them during the clear
light of day! What consternation it would cause."[21] From this in-
sight the protagonist goes on to the assertion that Dr. Bledsoe (like
Hulan Jack, drinker of Thunderbird), also eats chitterlings, in private,
however.

In section two of the poem, the speaker gives additional emphasis to the difficulty the would-be assimilationist has in becoming
a faceless member of the majority. The ambiguous voice of this section is that of the urbane artist and primitive hunter (simultaneously
so). The tension of this surrealistic section reflects the psychic
trauma of the black middle class.

The third and fifth sections introduce attacks on black groups
motivated by the assimilationist dream. The "firemasons," a black
group evidently based on the principles of white masonic orders, and
primarily concerned with appearance, parades, and regalia, are first
condemned. In the fifth section, the black church is attacked. This
is given further treatment in the play *The Baptism*, which must be
seen as a statement on religion in general.

The sixth section "die schwartze Bohemien" is crucial to the
poem. This segment works in much the same way that the passages
of self-deprecation worked in the shorter poems. Here, the vacuous

mouthings of the typical black inhabitant of the Village must be seen as representative of the mind of the poet himself. Lacking the capacity for belief of any kind,

> [. . .] religion was something
> he fount in coffee shops, by God.

he has only excuses for not communicating with black people and committing himself to their struggles, whether in the South,

> It's not that I got enything
> against cotton, nosiree, by God
> It's just that . . .

or merely Harlem.

> It's just that it's such a drag to go
> way uptown for Bar B Cue,
>   By God . . .

The anguish of this self-condemnation must surely be recalled when we examine the dramatic shift, the return to "uptown," of 1965. This self-indictment somewhat softens the final blistering attack on the sister, but only slightly.

The final section of "Hymn . . ." begins with a litany which the poet, apparently with tongue in cheek, dedicates to those blacks entrapped in the worship of whiteness. The section begins:

> About my sister.
>   (O, generation revered
>   above all others.
>   O, generation of fictitious
>   Ofays
>   I revere you . . .
>   You are all so beautiful)

The poem continues with a rapid cataloguing of the flaws of his materialistically oriented, appearance-mad, self-hating sister:

> my sister drives a green jaguar
> my sister has her hair done twice a month

[. . .]
My sister doesn't like to teach in Newark
    because there are too many colored
    in her classes
[. . .]
my sister's boyfriend is a faggot music teacher
    who digs Tschaikovsky
my sister digs Tschaikovsky also
[. . .] they will probably get married.
    Smiling & glad/in
    the huge & loveless
    white-anglo sun/of
    benevolent step
    mother America.

The poet's sister has become a gross exaggeration of her models, her self-deception surpassing even that of the black Bohemien. It is important to note here that the poet sees this self-deception as just that, *i.e. self*-deception. Whereas, in the later works such behavior would be interpreted as racial betrayal, in this early poem race is approached in a more existential manner. The individual, faced constantly with the forces of convention, must hold on to some sense of self at all costs. Race, at this point of the writer's development divorced from nationalistic thought, is another one of those precious few distinguishing factors. Finally, this poem, in spite of the reference to "step mother America," should not be read as evidence of the poet's acceptance of "mother Africa." A consideration of the final poem of the collection, "Notes for a Speech," should quickly dispel such an assumption.

In "Notes for a Speech," the poet speaks of his separation from the people of Africa. He shows here an attitude diametrically opposed to that of his more recent works, wherein he vigorously posits the essential Africanness of all black Americans. The poet concludes that this distant land and its people have little, if anything, in common with him and he must face up to the reality of his existence as product of the new world:

    [. . .] My color
    is not theirs. Lighter, white man
    talk. They shy away. My own
    dead souls, my, so called

people. Africa
is a foreign place. You are
as any other man here
american.

Preface, then, ends with the "American" poet ambiguously confronting his national identity, highly critical of the nation, yet accepting
its claim on him. Not yet able to find the moral direction so desired
and momentarily felt in "Betancourt," the poet reverts to the brooding hopelessness of the earlier poems. *Preface to a Twenty Volume
Suicide Note*, "mosaic of disorder," closes with the poet's acceptance
of his ineffectuality, the last lines seeming to serve as a justification
for his Beat withdrawal.

The poems of *Preface* attest to the extent of Baraka's debt to
William Carlos Williams and Charles Olson. The poet publicly
acknowledged this debt as early as 1959 in a short statement entitled
"How You Sound?" published in Donald M. Allen's *New American
Poetry 1945-1960*. In this essay the poet says:

> I make a poetry with what I feel is useful & can be saved out of all the
> garbage of our lives. What I see, am touched by (CAN HEAR) . . . wives,
> gardens, jobs, cement yards where cats pee, all my interminable arti-
> facts . . . ALL are a poetry, & nothing moves (with any grace) pried apart
> from these things. There cannot be a closet poetry. Unless the closet be
> as wide as God's eye
>
> . . . . There must not be any preconceived notion or *design* for what the
> poem *ought* to be. 'Who knows what a poem ought to sound like? Until
> it's thar' Says Charles Olson . . . & I follow closely with that. I'm not
> interested in writing sonnets, sestinas or anything . . . only poems. . . .
> The only 'recognizable tradition' a poet need to follow is himself . . .
> & with that, say, all those things out of tradition he can use, adapt, work
> over, into something for himself. To broaden his *own* voice with. (You
> have to start and finish there . . . your own voice . . . how you sound.)
>
> . . . we want to go into a quantitative verse . . . the 'irregular foot' of
> Williams . . . the 'Projective verse' of Olson. Accentual verse, the regular
> metric of rumbling iambics, is dry as slivers of sand. Nothing happens in
> that frame anymore. We can get nothing from England and the diluted
> formalism of the academy (the formal culture of the U.S.) is anaemic &
> fraught with incompetence & unreality.[22] (1959)

In this particular statement and in a later interview with *Nomad/New York* magazine,[23] the poet mentions the early influence of Eliot, whose academicism, finally, does not interest him. He also mentions the influence of Lorca, whose exoticism he feels aided him in escaping the strong attraction of the Eliotian mode. Pound, too, by the poet's admission, was a dominant influence. In the *Nomad/New York* interview, he says: "From Pound I learned some of the things that went into imagist poetry, the idea of the image and what it ought to be. I learned probably about verse from Pound—how a poem should be made, what a poem ought to look like— an inkling anyway. . . ." He ends this interview, however, with another bouquet to his more compelling mentor. He says, ". . . from Williams (I learned), I guess how to get it out in my own language."

Baraka shows his kinship to Williams, first of all, in the frequent homeliness of his subject matter. Like the earlier poet, Baraka is concerned with breaking down the barriers between that which is considered worthy of poetic treatment and that which is not. It is this attitude that allows him to include elements from the "low brow" realms of comic strip, radio, and movies in his verse. These things, like "old junkies" ("Way Out West") and radio disk jockeys ("Symphony Sid"), are all his "interminable artifacts," and it is the poet's contention that the poetry or art which refuses to deal with such subjects is an art of lies.

Baraka seems to have taken to heart William's statement from *Paterson* concerning "the line" and the means of invigorating it. Williams says:

Without invention nothing is well spaced,
unless the mind change, unless
the stars are new measured, according
to their relative position, the
line will not change, [. . .] unless there is
a new mind there cannot be a new
line, the old will go on
repeating itself with recurring
deadliness: [. . .]
[. . .]

> without invention the line
> will never again take on its ancient
> divisions when the word, a supple word,
> lived in it, crumbled now to chalk.[24]

An examination of the poems of *Preface* will show immediately the highly inventive or improvisational nature of Baraka's early verse. His form varies from the almost "closed" verse of the title poem of the collection to the prosaic lines of "Vice," from the lyrical lines of "The Clearing" to the truncated lines of "Way Out West," from the Whitmanesque sweep of "One Night Stand" to the taut lines of "Betancourt." There are also poems that include all these styles. "Hymn for Lanie Poo" is perhaps the most striking example of the latter. In any event, the works are generally evidence of the poet's attempt to find forms compatible with content, a central tenet in Olson's doctrine of "Projective Verse."

The poems are also exemplary of the writer's employment of speech rhythms. Marked by discontinuities and frequent syntactic difficulties, the works show a concern with language as it is spontaneously set down, or "breathed" (to use Olson's term) by its creator. This difficulty of snytax, though one of the poet's aids in achieving the effect of spontaneity, is, on the other hand, one of his most glaring flaws in that it so often brings forth an almost inaccessible poetry. This is also the major problem with the extreme privacy of the writer's allusions. Yet, even as we bring these complaints to the poems, we do so with the feeling that this poet's turbulent experience could only be expressed in a poetry of discontinuities, frequent syntactic difficulties, and coded allusion. The poem "Titles," from *The Dead Lecturer* (to be discussed in chapter two) provides us with all the apology needed for the poems of *Preface.*

> My head
> is a fine
> tangle. My soul, a
> quick note, settled
> in the flesh.
> There are so many lyrics,
> so many
> others
> who will not understand.

I will say this to you tho,
It is not as if
there were
any more beautiful
way.

The Baptism and *The Toilet*

Whereas the earliest poems of Baraka, built on the "terrible disorder of a young man," are primarily self-accusatory, the earliest plays are primarily indictments of conventional society and its institutions. Both *The Baptism* and *The Toilet* are concerned with ritualized or codified behavior and its invitable end result, the stifling of love. Although *The Baptism* was first presented on March 23, 1964, only one day before the premier of *Dutchman, Dutchman*, to be discussed in the following chapter, is obviously a more mature work. Like *The Toilet*, with which it was first published in 1967, *The Baptism* appears to have been written as early as 1961, the year in which the Playright's Unit of Actor's Studio presented an off-Broadway production of *The Toilet*. The writing of *The Baptism* would seem to antedate even this performance.

The Baptism shows some of the same concerns as *Preface*, but in his vigorous attempt to exorcise conventional morality, materialism, and the rejection of the full life, the dramatist almost lets his blasphemous exuberance get the better of him. This tendency has led to overly harsh critical treatment of the play. Donald P. Costello, commenting on *The Baptism*, says: "Jones strains to be shocking, and the play ends up to be incoherent and adolescent, with scatter-shot fury."[25] In view of the "campy" excesses and the seemingly gratuitous profanity and sex in the play, Costello's indictment, at first glance, appears to be fairly judicious. However, a more exacting study of *The Baptism* reveals remarkable compatibility of form and content. The raucous language and sexual emphasis work as exorcism in reverse. Ritualized "obscenity" is used to destroy the language as well as the practice of restraint, which is the only real perversion. The same can be said of *The Toilet*, which even goes beyond *The*

Baptism is its freedom of expression and employment of the sexual.

The thematic relationship of these two works is seen most clearly in their treatment of homosexuality, a central issue in both plays. Baraka, much like Baldwin in these early works, uses the homosexual metaphorically. Denied admission to the "straight" world, the homosexual is forced to live the life of the outsider. This is his bane as well as his blessing. On the one hand, he is not bound by the dehumanizing strictures of the majority culture. This exclusion is, nevertheless, the cause of tremendous suffering. On the other hand, the homosexual gains through his apprenticeship in suffering. Instead of becoming embittered by his experience, he achieves spiritual maturity. Hence, homosexuality, at least in the works under consideration, is seen as a liberating force. Because he is able to love, to respond openly to his fellows in a hate-filled and closed world, the homosexual of Baraka's early works is, ironically, a better "man" than the "straights" around him. Through the homosexuals of *The Baptism* and *The Toilet*, the dramatist seems to be showing us just how "queer" it is for one to break the taboo against tenderness in our modern toilet of a world. Ginsberg also uses this metaphor. Note the humorous, punning use of it in the conclusion of "America," his poetic harangue against a wrong-headed nation. Madly intent on injecting some love into a hate-filled and dying land, the speaker of the poem ends by saying that he is putting his "queer shoulder" to the wheel.[26]

The action of *The Baptism* takes place in "an almost well-to do arrogant Protestant church, obviously Baptist." Although the published text refers to the race of only one character, the messenger, we know, by implication, that the other characters are black. First, we know by the gaudy decor of the pulpit. The gilded and velvet furnishings call to mind later indictments of the "faboulous" (sic) churches of middle class blacks. (See "The Screamers" in *Tales*.) We know also by the unflattering picture of the minister, which becomes particularly scathing in the later *Slave Ship*. The songs of the worshippers, spirituals, also reinforce our awareness of the racial indentities of the characters. The same effect is achieved through reference to such figures as Marcus Garvey, the black nationalist leader of the 1920's. These and other aspects of the drama would inform the reader of the racial makeup of the characters, even if he did not know that the play was performed with black actors in 1964. The employment of black characters has led some commentators to see this early work as simply a statement of the evil, anesthetizing influence of the black church, *i.e.*, the black church as "opiate of the (black) people." However, *The Baptism* is a much more general statement on religion as practiced in an excessively prohibitive American society. The play is a universal comment on a religion that breeds hypocrisy, guilt, restraint, and hatred in the hearts of its practitioners. The dramatist, in making the statement, simply draws on the existence of the malaise in the setting that he knows best, *i.e.*, the black Baptist church.

The play may very well be a parody of such elements of the Christian faith as the concept of the Trinity and the judgement. However, to focus on this aspect alone is to ignore the central concern of the drama. It is to ignore the key methaphorical implications of the church and the characters' attitudes concerning sex. The church is the embodiment of the controlling institutions of the society. It upholds those values which advance the group while they simultaneously stifle individual potential. The characters reveal their accommodation or rejection to society's mandates through their sexuality. The central crisis of the drama is seen in the boy's conflict with the elders and their institutions.

The destructive nature of their ethics is seen to best advantage in the actions of the minister and the female characters of the play. The minister, self-righteous and greedy, is described in this manner: "Black robe, white haired, pompous, appears well meaning, generally ridiculous." He is guardian of man's repressive institutions and his remarks are fittingly reminiscent of Blake's Nobodaddy. He moans:

> Break the chain of ignorance. Lord in his high place. What returns to us. Images, the tone of death. Our cloak of color, our love for ourselves and our hymns... Not love [...] Not love. The betrayed music. Stealth. We rise to the tops of our buildings and they name them after us. We take off our hoods [...] and show our eyes. I am holy father of silence.

Instead of breaking the chains of ignorance, the minister binds his flock more securely in the fetters of hatred ("not love"), secrecy, and restraint. His selfishness is best seen in his comment, "I fuck no one who does not claim to love me." In this assertion the minister, vibrant cocksman that he, shows, nevertheless, his spiritual impotence. In terms of the play, the minister's perversion and his conventional "faith" are inseparable. The homosexual shows his awareness of this when he indicts the minister with the stinging line, "You are filthy with success, you religious mother-fucker."

Another perversion is seen in the female characters of the play. They seek to repress the libido through complete absorption in the church. That they are not wholly successful is evident in the old woman's description of the central character's, the boy's, masturbation. She says:

> He sinned, He sinned. He sinned [. . .] I saw him. I watched him kneel and blaspheme our God. Sin, Sin. A demon of hot flesh [. . .] Sin. He closed his eyes. The lashes fluttered. [. . .] BLASPHEMER. You spilled your seed while pretending to talk to God. I saw you. That quick short stroke. And it was soft before and you made it grow in your hand. I watched it stiffen [. . .] The flesh. My God. Those lovely eyelids moving. [. . .] My lovely, lovely youth. (*She collapses trying to grab the boy's legs.*)

The old woman tried in vain to restrain her human, fleshly desires. She, the young women of the drama, and all other followers of conventional morality are doomed to suffer unnecessary guilt and anguish until they learn the lesson of the homosexual, who incessantly sings a panegyric to complete experience and intuitive knowledge.

> The pride of life is life. And flesh must make its move. I am the sinister lover of love. The mysterious villain of thought. I love my mind, my asshole too. I love all things. As they are issued from you know who. God. God. Go-o-d.

He later adds to this Blakean/Whitmanesque/Ginsbergian comment, "The devil is part of creation like any ash tray or senator. Why segregate him?" In the mind of the homosexual, who speaks for the Zen-inspired Beatnik, "Everything that lives is holy." Scornful of the rapacious egotism of the minister as well as the repressed anxieties of the old woman, he shows us that his God is the God of experiential, outer-directed excess.

Come commentators, salesmen, radicals, let no one say we have not tried
to be everything. Let no one say we have not fucked everything and
everyone we could. Let no one say we failed the spirit of the Renaissance. I be Giotto of the queers. I be Willie Mays of the queers. I not be
lim-lim-limited by tiny nigger songs. Dance with me boy.

The invitation is crucial. This farce comes as close to tragedy as possible in the implications of the boy's rejection of the homosexual,
whose invitation represents the call to full humanity. As scion of
"straight" society, however, the boy is torn between the negative forces of the old woman and the minister, both parental figures. We see
their influence in the boy's guilt concerning his masturbation. We
see, in his violent outburst, a final intolerance of the frustrations of
the repressed libidinal urge. His self-righteous and neurotic act of ven-
geance is fraught with symbolic meaning. The "long silver sword" is
metaphor for the fleshly tool which his elders, in the interest of society, have forbidden him to use.

The only survivor of the boy's wrath is the homosexual. Kick-
ed aside by the Christians for attempting to protect the boy, he manages to remain undetected at the height of the fury. The play makes
its final comment on the evils of convention by juxtaposing the
actions of its practitioners against the actions of the homosexual.
Not only do we see his true worth in his "blasphemous" remarks. We
see also, in his earlier attempts to halt the bloodshed, that he is the
only character with any understanding whatsoever of true charity.
Automatically an outsider in the eyes of the general society, he is not
bound by its dictates, especially those concerning sex roles. It is his
conviction that he is no less a man for responding with a tenderness
devoid of guilt. Nor does he feel his manhood diminished because he
chooses not to destroy others. His concerns are with love and life
throughout the drama. It is no wonder, then, that he sees mass death
as merely "some uninteresting kind of orgy." Savoring all experience,
hating restraint, hypocrisy and greed, the homosexual manifests key
aspects of the Beat psyche. This work, however, does not approach
the depth of feeling found in *Preface*. Neither does the early play
The Toilet, though it is in some ways an improvement.

The Toilet, according to the Grove Press edition, was first presented at St. Mark's Playhouse, New York, on December 16, 1964.

However, as I have noted above, there is evidence that it was performed as early as 1961. Moveover, the following lines from the poem "Look for You Yesterday. . . . ," discussed earlier, would lead us to believe that the play was written before the publication of *Preface* (1961):

> Was James Karolis a great sage??
> Why did I let Ora Mathews beat him up
> in the bathroom? Haven't I learned my lesson

Here, at least three years before the St. Mark's production of the play, we see the names of the characters as well as a capsule reference to the crucial event of the work. The highly symbolic nature of the names would seemingly negate any claim that the poet was merely recalling a real life experience later transformed into dramatic art. *The Toilet* was formally conceived as early as 1961, during the early days of Baraka's involvement with the Village scene.

This play derives much of its power from Baraka's faithful presentation of the experiences of the adolescent boy. The writer's ability in this area is seen again, and perhaps to best advantage, in the stories of *Tales*. Everything *belongs* in this extremely naturalistic play. The earthy language, rivaling even that heard in *The Baptism*, is a real and necessary part of this world of young, primarily black, urban school boys. The language of *The Toilet* emphasizes the intense but misguided efforts of these adolescents to assert their manhood. Likewise, the setting, a "large bare toilet of gray rough cement . . ." and resembling "the impersonal ugliness of a school toilet or a latrine of some institution," is right for this work. The setting is symbol of our bleak and viciously regulated world. In retrospect, even the strong introductory stage directions do not seem excessive. The play opens with these instructions: *"The actors should give the impression frequently that the place smells."* After seeing one of the actors urinate into one of the commodes, *"spraying urine over the seat,"* we are ready for the first lines of *The Toilet*.

As pointed out by Paul Witherington in "Exorcism and Baptism in LeRoi Jones's *The Toilet*,"[27] the boys wish to show their masculinity by discarding all maternal or "soft" values. At the same time, however, they are driven to find means of expressing love within the group. Consequently, the boys have a real need for affection as well as a fear of the demands of love. Their thwarted libidinal urge is expressed in the form of violence. The dialogue, often funny and firmly rooted in the black idiom, not only focuses on universally identifiable character types (the bully, the coward, the "signifier"). It simultaneously probes the various ways by which the boys enforce the taboo against tenderness.

Driven to deny impulses which they consider "unmanly," the boys exhibit hostility in varying forms throughout the play. These actions culminate in the desperate actuality of physical violence against Karolis. However, the violence takes a more subtle appearance in the early stages of the drama. The boys engage in name-calling and the well known ghetto game, "the dozens," at the start of the action. Both activities serve to shield the participants from the greatly feared overt expression of love, an expression that is ironically manifested in the very need for the gang. Yet, the boys feel that as long as they can call one another "bastid" or "cocksucka," they remain safely within the boundaries of masculine behavior. The same motivating factor is in evidence in the playing of "the dozens," a game in which the participants exchange slurs about one another's parents. The slurs are usually of a sexual nature and directed against the mother. Witherington is perhaps correct in seeing this game as additional evidence that the boys are attempting to exorcise maternal values. It is no less indicative of their desire to show their hardness, their ability to give and take the most crushing blows short of actual violence. The winner of "the dozens" competition is invariably the "man" who through his sheer poetic skill and bawdy imagination can force his opponent to actual violence, or worse, tears (See "The Death of Horatio Alger" in *Tales*.).

Although repressed behavior is seen in all the boys, with the exceptions of Karolis and Farrell, it is most glaringly present in the brutal Ora. Ora evinces an absolute horror of compassion, and justly so. If we consider the controlling metaphor for love in the drama, *i.e.*., homosexuality Ora shows himself most vulnerable to its expression. We see it, first, in his frequently invoked appellations ("cocksucka," "dick licker"). He, furthermore, attempts to engage in oral sex with Karolis and is only interrupted by Ray's entrance. Ora is a latent homosexual. In terms of the metaphorical implications of the play, however, he has a tremendous desire to express love. Because his world does not allow this expression, he inverts his desire. While the callous Oras can live with this necessary inversion, the sensitive Rays cannot.

Foots/Ray is Baraka's earliest presentation of the skinny, intelligent, bug-eyed, middle-class black boy who figures so prominently in the author's writings. We see him as a young child in "Uncle tom's Cabin: Alternate Ending" (*Tales*). In some of the stories, even the name Ray is used. Much of the writer's own life went into these various portraits.

Ray is the middle-class black boy who is torn between two cultures. The dramatist's description of him as "manic" is not extreme. His psychic trauma stems from the schizoid nature of his existence. His problem will be articulated later by Clay in *Dutchman*. We get our first glimpse of Ray's problem and the boys' understanding of it in Hines's statement concerning Ray's whereabouts. Hines says:

> I think he's still in Miss Powell's class. You know if he missed her class she'd beat his head, and then get his ol' lady to beat his head again.

The white teachers take a special interest in Ray because he is "one" worth saving. The other boys are lost causes. The knowledge of his special treatment causes Ray intense feelings of guilt. Hence, his tremendous desire to belong to his black peers. His feeble attempts to laugh at this situation only serve to intensify our appreciation of his pain:

> That goddamn Van Ness had me in his office. He said I'm a credit to my race. (*Laughs and all follow.*) He said I'm smart-as-a-whip (*imitating Van Ness*) and should help him to keep all you unsavory (*again imitating*) elements in line. (*All laugh again*).

This halting laughter reveals the insecurity of all concerned. Ray is whiter. His homelife most assuredly is closer to that of the teachers than to the black peers. His good grades are sure to lead him to college and a comfortable niche in mainstream society. His upwardly mobile mother, the sterotypical Yiddish mother in blackface, will be there to counter every backsliding move on his part. In spite of these things, he manages to hold onto his role as leader. He does it through sheer intellectual prowess and the actor's ability to project a consummate "macho" image, which is all the more important to Ray because of his fragile physique.

Whereas the gang will tolerate a bourgeois intellectual as a leader, it will never accept a leader whose masculinity is in doubt. Consequently, Ray must deny his relationship with Karolis in order to belong. He must be Foots, not Ray. At the height of the fury, Karolis tells the gang members as much:

> [...] his name is Ray, not Foots. You stupid bastards. I love somebody you don't even know.

Karolis understands that his lover is "Foots" only when he surrenders to the gang's debased concept of manhood. The nickname itself implies a plodding, lock-stepped entanglement. "Ray," on the other hand, implies freedom and the light of the spirit, able to shine only when free of the restraining pressures of the group.

The Toilet, despite its violence and ugliness, does conclude on an optimistic note. After the climactic confrontation, the boys leave Karolis bleeding on the urine-soaked toilet floor. Ray manages to sneak back to his side undetected. The play ends in silence, but with the following stage directions: *". . . the door is pushed open slightly, then it opens completely and FOOTS comes in. He stares at Karolis' body for a second, looks quickly over his shoulder then runs and kneels before the body, weeping and cradling the head in his arms."* In this markedly maternal gesture, Ray rejects the "macho" role demanded by the gang and asserts another understanding of "manhood." The real man is again the individual with the strength to divorce himself from the inhibiting influence of the majority. In these early works that individual is the homosexual. In the ensuing works the black American takes over this role, as Baraka becomes increasingly convinced that "any black American, simply by virtue of his blackness is weird, a nonconformist in this society."28

Though this play has little explicit to say concerning the issue of race, the final scene causes some critics to see the whole work as a statement on race relations. Even Baraka himself seems to have forgotten the real issue of the play. Speaking of the conclusion, he says:

> When I first wrote the play, it ended with everybody leaving. I tacked the other ending on; the kind of social milieu that I was in dictated the kind of rapprochment. It actually did not evolve from the pure spirit of the play. I've never changed it of course, because I feel that now that would only be cute. I think you should admit where you were even if it's painful, but you should also understand your development and growth. . . . But that was ground that I walked on and covered, I can't deny it now.[29]

Baraka is, of course, right in saying that the Beat milieu dictated the concluding scene, but he is wrong in implying that "that kind of rapprochment" should be read "racial rapprochment." Were Karolis black or Ray white, the play would carry the same thematic weight. Basically, *The Toilet* is no more concerned with race than is *The Baptism*. A measure of the writer's total involvement in his milieu is seen in his ability to populate his works with blacks and whites, even in conflict, and yet not be obsessed with race as central theme.

Although *The Baptism* and *The Toilet* are obviously products of the same period in the writer's development, their dissimilarity in style is worthy of comment. *The Baptism* is in no way an attempt at "representational" drama. Markedly expressionistic in technique, the work is evidence of the writer's awareness of the absurdists, who gained prominence in the '50's and '60's. Like the works of the absurdists, *The Baptism* is a conscious rejection of realistic theatre. This anti-realism is effected in a number of ways. First, the existence of the characters as "believable" examples of everyday humanity is purposely undercut by their lack of personal names. Minister, boy, old woman, *etc.* bear testimony to the depersonalizing consequences of modern society. The fragmented, often nonsensical, speech of the characters, strikingly similar to some of the more private lyrics of Baraka, is exemplary of the conscious cacophony of the absurdists. The general effect of distortion and unreality is enhanced also by the abundance of raw sounds, especially "moaning" and "screaming." Because of these and other effects, *The Baptism* frequently approaches the realm of cartoon. The humor is, however, balanced by the viewer's unsettling knowledge that the play images the chaos of his own life. Finally, *The Baptism*, like the best works of the absurdists, is impervious to any definitive analysis. The play, like the world of which it is a part, refuses to yield an absolutely logical meaning. This is not the case with *The Toilet.*

The Toilet is a drama of extreme realism, or naturalism. Everything about the play is intended to enhance the viewer's belief in the actuality of the situation. The setting is of extreme importance in that it grounds the viewers in the tactile. Indeed it is no accident that Baraka emphasizes the solidity of the scene (*"The scene is a large bare toilet built of gray rough cement."*). Like the setting, the other aspects of the drama, characterization, diction, and action, express the same concreteness. The boys are all flesh and blood "types" with particular names. They also speak an understandable, earthy idiom. Furthermore, their actions, urinating intermittently, and giving the "impression frequently that the place smells," add to the viewer's illusion that he is secretly observing life in a public school "john" in all its squalor. *The Toilet*, unlike *The Baptism*, offers a meaning as explicit as its technique.

The starkly represented styles of these two works are rarely manifested so singularly in the writing to follow. Although the writer's subsequent method includes both avant-garde (witness the plays *Home on the Range* and *The Death of Malxolm X*) and realistic/naturalistic efforts (the story "Going down Slow"), his better work is a synthesis of the expressionistic and naturalistic modes.

In conclusion, whether reflecting the essential optimism of Ginsberg, as seen in the brief concluding scene of *The Toilet*, or the more nihilistic pessimism of Burroughs, seen throughout *Preface*, the early work is best understood in the context of the Beat movement. The following chapter will focus on the writer's growing discontent, embryonically present in *Preface*, and his final dissociation from these early influences.

Notes

[1] *Current Biography, 1970, p. 204.*

[2] Interview with Judy Stone, "If It's Anger . . . Maybe That's Good," *San Francisco Chronicle*, 23 August 1964, pp. 39, 42.

[3] *Ibid.*, 42

[4] LeRoi Jones, "Salute," in *Tales* (New York: Grove Press, 1967), p. 82.

[5] Isabel Eberstadt, "King of the East Village," *New York Herald Tribune*, 12 December 1964, Sunday Magazine Section, pp. 13-15, 18, 20.

[6] Clellon Holmes, *New York Times*, 16 November 1952, Magazine Section, p. 10

[7] Norman Mailer, "The White Negro," *Advertisements for Myself* (New York: Putnam, 1959), p. 339.

[8] Gene Feldman, *The Beat Generation and the Angry Young Men* (New York: Citadel Press, 1958), p. 10.

[9] William Fischer, "The Pre-Revolutionary Writings of Imamu Amiri Baraka," *Massachusetts Review* XIV, 2 (13 July 1973): 259-305.

[10] *Ibid.*, 270

[11] LeRoi Jones, *Kulchur*, vol. 3, no. 9 (Spring, 1963): 96.

[12] Fischer, 265.

[13] Denise Levertov, *Nation* CXCIII (14 October 1961): 251.

[14] Jack Newfield, "The Beat Generation and the Un-Generation," *America Changing* (Columbus, Ohio: 1968), p. 268.

[15] Lee Jacobus, "Imamu Amiri Baraka: the Quest for Moral Order," in

Modern Black Poets, ed: Donald Gibson (Englewood Cliffs, N. J.: Prentice-Hall, Inc., 1973), p. 119.

16Allen Ginsberg, *Prose Contribution to Cuban Revolution* (Detroit: Artists' Workshop Press, 1966), n.p.

17LeRoi Jones, "Cuba Libre," in *Home: Social Essays* (New York: William Morrow and Company, 1966), p. 42.

18*Ibid.*, 42.

19*Ibid.*, 20.

20*Ibid.*, 61.

21Ralph Ellison, *Invisible Man* (New York: New American Library (Signet), 1952), p. 230.

22LeRoi Jones, "How You Sound," in *New American Poetry*, ed: Donald Allen (New York: Grove Press, 1960), pp. 424-25.

23Interview with *Nomad/New York* (Autumn, 1962): pp. 20-22.

24William Carlos Williams, "Sunday in the Park," from Paterson, Book II (New York: New Directions, 1963), p. 50.

25Donald Costello, "Black Man as Victim," in *Five Black Writers*, ed: Donald Gibson (New York: New York University Press, 1970), p. 207.

26Allen Ginsberg, "America," *Howl* (San Francisco, 1973), 34.

27Paul Witherington, "Exorcism and Baptism in LeRoi Jones's The Toilet," *Modern Drama* 15 (September, 1972): pp. 159-163.

28LeRoi Jones, "City of Harlem," *Home* (New York: Morrow, 1966), p. 93.

29Mel Watkins, "Talk with LeRoi Jones," *New York Times Book Review*, 27 June 1971, p. 26.

Chapter II

Joseph To His Brothers

I am deaf and blind and lost and will not again sing your quiet verse.
     I have lost
even the act of poetry, and writhe now for cool horizonless dawn.

LeRoi Jones is a poet, is a teacher, is a playwright, is a critic, is a celeb-
rity, is a king of the lower East Side. Is a Flaming Seducer, is a Rabid
Racist, who Hates whites, Hates Negroes, Hates Homosexuals, Hates
intellectuals, Hates liberals, and Watch Out, he's a killer![1]

Isabel Eberstadt's tongue in cheek comment, from her December 1964 article "King of the East Village," is an indication of Baraka's emergence as "personality" during the early 1960's. To be sure,
Eberstadt indicates in the remainder of her highly favorable article,
that the LeRoi Jones of her acquaintance was quite different from
the LeRoi Jones of the press and popular reputation. In fact, she
tries to disprove some of the sensational rumors by noting that the
poet was happily married to a Jewish intellectual at the time. There
were, nevertheless, those outraged detractors who would have agreed
with Eberstadt's introductory statement, completely missing her
rather obvious levity. Baraka's fiery reputation grew with the appear-
ances of his increasingly political and race-conscious publications and
theatrical productions. The poetry, drama, fiction, and social essays
written between 1961 and 1965 are evidence of the poet's protracted
assimilation of the crucial Cuban experience. Evidence of the influence of this experience is most graphically seen in the works to be
considered in this chapter, all of which were written after 1960. Although we perceive the quickening influence of the Cuban trip in at
least two poems of *Preface*, the experience plays no major part in
most of the poems, some of which were written as early as 1957. The
largely self-directed anger of the poems of *Preface* is still present to
some degree, but the later work is primarily directed to the liberal
and apolitical artist friends of the poet. The works are, however, as

much self-explanation on the part of the poet as they are indictments of his associates.

Perhaps the best treatment of Baraka's activities following the climactic Cuban visit is found in Harold Cruse's *The Crisis of the Negro Intellectual* (1967). Cruse, himself a member of the visiting black group, gives his own version of the trip, which affords us an interesting sidelight on the prose account given by Baraka in "Cuba Libre."

Cruse says:

> In his article about his trip, "Cuba Libre," [Jones] wrote mockingly of certain individuals in the writers' contingent as being "nineteen-forty-ish" and "nineteen thirtyish" (as if to say that the really "in" thing was to be "nineteen-fiftyish.") Jones was also disappointed by the fact that many "name" writers he was eager to meet did not accept the invitation to Cuba with him. . . . At any rate, his actual experience in Cuba amply compensated Jones for the lack of representative Negro writers in his delegation.[2]

The ample compensation was, of course, the tremendously unsettling, finally inspirational, effect of the trip, as evidenced in "One Night Stand" and "Betancourt." The poet's all-consuming desire to sever his relationship with the apolitical village milieu was quickened by: (1) his flattering first-hand experience (as emissary for oppressed blacks in America) with the Cuban revolutionaries and (2) his meeting with Robert Williams, the civil rights leader from Monroe, North Carolina. Williams inflamed the minds of many nascent revolutionaries and nationalistically oriented blacks of the 1950's by his militant opposition to harassment by the Ku Klux Klan. In Cuba, then, Baraka met face-to-face with persons who, in his mind, represented purpose and direction. They had done in the real world what the poet had thought possible only in the worlds of comic strip fantasy.

Baraka decided that Robert Williams, Fidel Castro, and the young writers he met in Cuba would serve as his models. Evidence of his attempt to put their teachings into practice is seen in his growing socio-political involvement following the Cuban trip. Unlike the "schwartze bohemien" of "Hymn for Lanie Poo," the poet became intensely involved for the first time with the "Uptown" scene.

According to Cruse, Baraka created his first Harlem-based organization, the "On Guard for Freedom Committee," in 1961. This group,
composed of blacks from Harlem as well as whites from Baraka's
older Village group, the "Organization of Young Men," was primarily
concerned with supporting Williams to the extent of sending muni-
tions to Monroe, North Carolina. This scheme failed for reasons best
explained by Cruse. I cite the design merely to show the intensity of
the poet's developing revolutionary zeal. This fervor is reflected in
the many social essays that Baraka produced during this period.
These prose pieces, most of which were later collected in *Home:
Social Essays* (1966), originally appeared in such journals as *Mid-
stream, Saturday Review, Nation, Negro Digest, The Liberator* and
others. They show either intense disfavor with the gradualism of the
Civil Rights Movement or a budding cultural nationalism. *Blues
People* (1963), his most significant work in the social realm, was
written during this period.

   In spite of his activities in Harlem, the poet was still very much
a "mover" on the artistic Village scene. His poems, of course, continued to appear in underground journals such as *Floating Bear* and
Fuck You/A Magazine of the Arts, both of which he edited or co-
edited. They also began to appear in such journals as *Harper's, Massachusetts Review, The Nation, Poetry, Evergreen Review*, and *The
Yale Literary Magazine*, to name only a few. This period saw also the
first published fiction of Baraka. His stories appeared in *The Moderns*
(1963), an anthology of experimentalist fiction edited by Baraka and
including works of members of the Village coterie. Baraka's fiction
also appeared in such journals as *Transatlantic Review* and *Evergreen
Review*. The writer's only effort in novel form, *The System of
Dante's Hell* (1963), was written during this period. Perhaps the best
indication of his continued involvement and significance "Downtown" is seen in his theatrical output during this period. It was in
1964 that Baraka's play *Dutchman* won the "Obie" award (for best
off-Broadway play of the season). *The Toilet* and *The Baptism* followed the successful run of *Dutchman*. As stated earlier, both plays
represent the earliest tendencies of the writer. Though they both
have their own particular merits, they do not represent the post-
Cuban psyche of Baraka and seem to have been produced, at least
partially, in effort to capitalize on the enormous success of *Dutchman*. A fourth work, *The Slave*, also produced in 1964 is, on the

other hand, highly representative of the work of this period. In a number of ways, it closes the second phase of Baraka's dramatic reorientation.

In the intensity of his socio-political involvement and his continued literary creativity, we see that between 1961 and 1965 Baraka had one foot in Harlem and the other in the Village. Torn between the two scenes and their respective demands, he found himself yielding to the implacable pull of Harlem. His relationship with the young black artists, which I shall discuss later, makes this period even more complex. Baraka's literary works reflect the tremendous tension of this period in that all represent, to some degree, the writer's attempt at explaining his psychic switch to his downtown peers. Moreover, these works, which show the increasingly pervasive influence of the Afro-American experience, are evidence of the writer's earliest efforts to conjoin art and politics.

The poems of *The Dead Lecturer* are primarily addressed to the writer's friends in art, the Village coterie. These works are not, as Cheryl Lynn Munro says in "LeRoi Jones: A Man in Transition," ". . . very definitely geared toward the black *litterateurs.*"[3] On the contrary, the poems repeatedly attack and carry the burden of rationalization to the "white" *litterateurs.* In these works the poet solidifies his commitment to revolutionary action and chides his literary peers for what he sees as their apolitical decadence. The poems of *The Dead Lecturer* and *Sabotage* are marked by an ever-increasing use of Afro-American allusion as well. In this manner, Baraka tells the former associates that he has different ideals and speaks from a different frame of reference. It is this aspect of *The Dead Lecturer* that Richard Howard has in mind when he says, "In this new book of poems, the poet has become much surer of his own voice, much braver with it . . . for in wrestling with the solipsistic violence of his feelings, he appears to have discovered his identity . . ."[4] The persona of the lyrics is recognizably black. His concerns are largely racial, and, like the protagonists of the plays of this period, he takes on the "privileged" position of the black man in the hell of the West. He sees himself as the last moral voice in America and accepts this role as though it were divinely ordained.

In a discussion of the poems of *The Dead Lecturer*, there is no better starting point than the poem "I Substitute for the Dead Lecturer." This central lyric begins with a reference to the attitudes of the poet's friends, the artist-intellectuals, concerning his growing political interests.

> They have turned, and say that I am dying. That
> I have thrown
> my life
> away.

The same concern is evidenced in "A Poem Some People Will Have to Understand," collected in *Sabotage* (one of three volumes included in *Black Magic Poetry*) and written at about the same time as was "I Substitute. . . ." In "A Poem . . ." Baraka says, with wry humor:

> [. . .] I practice no industry.
> I am no longer a credit
> to my race.

These lines, like those of the first poem, are not representative of the sentiments of the poet, but of his artist friends, middle class blacks, and liberals in general. They are convinced that the poet has forfeited his promised place alongside Ralph Bunche, George Washington Carver, and Joe Louis (the "credits" of which I most vividly recall being reminded in my Alabama youth). Indeed, the poet lets us know throughout the poems of *The Dead Lecturer* and *Sabotage* that he has cast his lot with the "debits." In "I Substitute . . ." he also talks of this group and his new sense of obligation. The poet comes to the conclusion that he can give them no less a gift than himself. Surely his cold poetic gifts, coming to the writer in nightmarish recollection, are insufficient to the needs of the poor. He is even more explicit with regard to this theme, *i.e.* the inefficacy of disengaged artistry, in "A Poem Welcoming Jonas Mekas to America," printed in *Sabotage*. Again the poet wonders, "What kindness, what wealth" can he offer those most in need of it?

> Old niggers in time on the
> dreary street. Man, 50. . . woman, 50, drunk and falling in the street.
> I could say, looking at their lot, a poet has just made a note of your
> hurt.

This shattering attack on art and poetry as practiced by himself and his friends is typical of the work of Baraka at this point. With this in mind we come to realize that the "dead lecturer" is the departed poet or obsolete esthetician. The speaker who "substitutes" for him is painfully coming to terms with the demands of commitment, artistically as well as socially and politically. He approaches the new role with a sense of prophetic mission:

> The Lord has saved me
> to do this. The Lord
> has made me strong.
> I am as I must have
> myself. Against all
> thought, all music,
> all my soft loves.

This sense of prophecy, seen throughout the work of this period, is quite evident in "Joseph to His Brothers." The poet obviously identifies with the biblical figure sold into slavery by his brothers. It becomes equally obvious, in examination of the latter works of Baraka, that he sees himself—and blacks in general—coming into God's favor, like Joseph.

Along with his "soft loves," *i.e.*, isolated esthetic concerns, "thought," or overriding analysis, becomes increasingly villainous in Baraka's writings. Just as socio-political relevance is elevated in his later works, the primacy of the feelings is also vigorously asserted. Baraka sees both these elements as key aspects of the Afro-American style. In his intense assertion of these elements, we see the intensity of the poet's concern with the question of identity. "I Substitute . . ." ends:

> [. . .] I am frightened that
> the flame of my sickness will
> burn off my face. And leave
> the bones, my stewed black
> skull, an empty cage of failure.

All the themes touched upon in "I Substitute . . ." are present also in "Short Speech to My Friends." If anything, the statement is even more explicit in "Short Speech. . . ." Here the poet simultaneously

explains the magnetic pull of the black community and censures himself for his self-imposed alienation. He laments the time misspent.

> /The perversity
> of separation, isolation
> after so many years of trying to enter thier kingdoms.

"Their kingdoms" are populated by those artists who evince the attitude so repugnant to Jaime Shelley (see note 18 of Chapter I).
Baraka goes on to contrast the sterility of his former work and that
of his peers with the vitality of the forms of his new sources. He
says:

> The poor have become our creators. The black. The thoroughly
> ignorant.

He is rejecting the belief that "art is something that white men do,"
as he tells us in the introduction to *Home*.

It is no coincidence that some of Baraka's best writing on jazz
music was done during this period. The intensity of his concern with
the black American's musical expression and its ever-present socio-
cultural meaning is evidenced in the monumental study *Blues People*.
His deep involvement with music during this period is also seen in the
frequency of his contributions to *Down Beat*, his many record reviews for *Kulchur*, and his liner notes for several record albums. This
studious immersion in Afro-American music convinced the writer
that the most authentic of black artists, the musicians, received their
strength from an unswerving dedication to their non-imitative roots.
Baraka addresses himself to this issue in "The Myth of a Negro Literature," originally a speech given to the American Society for African
Culture, March 14, 1962. In this address, Baraka contrasts black writing to black music. He says:

> Negro music alone, because it drew its strengths and beauties out of the
> depth of the black man's soul, and because to a large extent its traditions
> could be carried on by the lowest classes of Negroes, has been able to
> survive the constant and willful dilutions of the black middle class.
> Blues and jazz have been the only consistent exhibitors of "Negritude" in
> formal American culture simply because the bearers of its tradition
> maintained their essential identies as Negroes.[5]

Black music, the creation of the poor, the black, and the ignorant (i.e., those trained in the school of life, not the academy) will be a model for his art. His writings will, from this point, evince a concern with salvaging his identity as a black man. They will, moreover, address themselves to the specific social placement of the black American.

Along with the music, there were other black creative forces that influenced Baraka's reorientation. One of the most important of these was exerted by the black writers of the lower East Side, the so-called *Umbra* poets, named for the journal in which they published their works. Diane Middlebrook describes them by contrasting them with the Beat movement. Her description, considered in light of Baraka's psychic ambivalence during this period, is quite pertinent. She says, "The early Sixties, for many Americans, was the period of the Beat Generation. Thinking back on its writers, most Americans remember the names of white men who gathered, however briefly, in San Francisco: Jack Kerouac, Allen Ginsberg, William Burroughs, Rexroth, Ferlinghetti. But at the same time on the Lower East Side of Manhattan, a large, diverse group of bohemian blacks was at work rediscovering the texts of black consciousness: LeRoi Jones (Imamu Baraka), Bob Kaufman, Ted Joans, David Henderson. . . ."[6] The *Umbra* poets were also described by Art Berger in his article "Negroes with Pens":

> Gathered about Umbra and its new quarterly are (*sic*) a group of poets wielding their pens like bayonets against the old ways and responding to a strong inner drive to bring their words to their people. These black bards, unlike their colleagues in the downtown coffee houses, have broken out of the inbred circuit of the *avant garde* and are reading the strong output of their muse in Harlem, Bedford-Stuyvesant, Long Island, in Y's, and galleries, libraries, colleges, P.T.A.'s, house parties and cocktail lounges. They are being referred to more and more as a New Renaissance.[7]

The *Umbra* poets, too, were the new creators, extolled by Baraka in "Short Speech. . . ." Already addressing themselves to the question of black survival in America, these writers, who formally organized in 1962, most assuredly affected Baraka. (Evidence of the intense political involvement of this group is seen in the fact that Julian Bond—then civil rights worker and now Georgia state legislator

—Tom Dent—later of Free Southern Theater and *Freedomways* magazine—were leading members). Baraka was indeed acquainted with
them and even exchanged ideas with them, but his primary allegiance
was with the white *avant garde*. It is interesting to note that Berger's
article, written during the height of the *Umbra* movement, does not
mention Baraka. Middlebrook's article, written after the poet was
recognized as the "Father of the Black Arts Movement," seems to be
more influenced by later events. At best, Baraka was on the pe-
riphery of the *Umbra* movement. The poems of *The Dead Lecturer*
evince tremendous guilt on this issue. The poet frequently chides
himself and his peers for the exclusive or inbred nature of their verse,
which is in direct contrast to the explicit verse of the emerging black
poets. The *Umbra* poets were, above all, concerned with communicating with the poor and the black. Baraka lets us know in no uncertain terms that he and his peers have shown no such desire. He
says in "Green Lantern's Solo":

> What we have created, is ourselves
> as heroes, as lovers, as disgustingly
> evil. As Dialogues with the soul, with
> the self, Selves, screaming furiously
> to each other. As the same fingers
> touch the same faces, as the same
> mouths close on each other. The killed
> is the killer, the loved the lover [. . .]
> Each idea a reflection of itself
> and all the ideas men have ever had. Truth, Lie, so close they defy
> inspection, and are built into autonomy by naive fools,
> who have no wish for wholeness or strength.

The effect of the repetition in these lines is not unlike the reitera-
tive fury of, say, a John Coltrane solo. Baraka himself describes the
typical Coltrane solo in the following manner: ". . . John Coltrane's
music is fanatically chordal. In his solos, Coltrane attacks each chord
and seems to almost want to separate each note of the chord (and its
overtones) into separate entities and suck out even the most minute
musical potential."[8] In the lines from "Green Lantern's Solo," Baraka attacks the "chord" of selfishness in a similar manner. Here he
thoroughly anatomizes selfishness by probing its constituent manifestations. In the poet's disgust with the incestuous nature of the
avant garde poets, we see the implied desire for the didactic, outer-

directed expression of the committed black poets. Indeed, the evil of self-involvement, of egotism, is one of the dominant themes of *The Dead Lecturer*.

The evil of "thought," or what Baraka later comes to speak of as "reflection," is also repeatedly attacked on the grounds that too much of it strifles action or "expression," a sacred word in the later writings. In "Balboa, the Entertainer," the poet chides himself for his expert but safely distant articulation of the problems of the poor and the black. Again he is gnawingly aware that he and his friends only *talk* a good game:

>   (The philosophers
> of need, of which
> I am lately
> one,
>   will tell you. "The People,"
> (and not think themselves
> liable
> to the same
> trembling flesh). I say now, "The People,"
> as some lesson repeated, now,
> the lights are off, to myself,
> as a lover, or at the cold wind.

The attack on reflection is even more vigorously manifested in the poems of *Sabotage*, which are, in some ways more compatible with the latter works of Baraka than are the poems of *The Dead Lecturer*, though they were composed during the same period. One glaring difference is the relative directness of the poems of *Sabotage*. Witness the explicit nature of the following indictment of "thought." In "The Burning General," the poet asks himself:

> Why are you so sophisticated? You used to piss and shit in your
> pants.
> Now you walk around *thinking* all the time, as if that sacred act
> would
> rewrite the world in bop talk, giving medals to every limping coon in
> creation.

In these lines we see the poet's increasing use of the street idiom. This is evident not only in the scatological slang but also in the reference to "every limping coon," *i.e.*, every hip-walking black man. The limp is simply another manifestation of the frequently incomprehensible (to whites) Afro-American sense of style. In the later poem "Dada Zodji," the poet says:

> When I was coolest
> they said I limped.

In yet another reference to the hip black gait (from *In Our Terribleness*), the poet says:

> (lil ol greylandy asked me if i was cripple
> i said yeh, i hurt my leg
> but her eyes was
> cripple man
> i was
> cool

The poet expands his indictment of cold intellectualism by making more direct statements on the moral impotence of his friends. They are repeatedly characterized as men who do not know what it is to feel, to experience life emotionally. Because of this inadequacy he speaks of them, himself included, in "This Is the Clearing I Once Spoke of" as "dead children of thought." The attack is more specific in "Green Lantern's Solo," where he cites:

> My friend, the lyric poet,
> who has never had an orgasm. My friend,
> the social critic, who has never known society,
> My friend who has thrown himself against the dignity of
> all human flesh [. . .]

In "The End of Man Is His Beauty,"the poet indicts his peers on similar grounds. Throughout the poems of *The Dead Lecturer*, Baraka posits a more humanistic direction, one that allows the feelings space in which to breathe. He comes to the conclusion that excessive reflection only serves to cloak spiritual and moral impotence. The closed group of *avant garde* poets exhibits behavior closely akin to that seen in the young gang members of *The Toilet*. Both groups band together and act out their various rituals because of a basic fear of love. The poets can no more allow real love to surface than can the boys in the play. It is not cool to care. Baraka's final rejection of this orientation is seen to best advantage in the "Crow Jane" poems and "Black Dada Nihilismus," in which he mythicizes both his old disengaged esthetic and the emerging one.

"Crow Jane" is one of the two sequencial poems of *The Dead Lecturer*. The other is "A Poem for Willie Best." In some ways they are the most successful pieces of the book. Grouped around one basic symbolic figure, they are surely the most coherently sustained works. "Crow Jane," a distillation of the crucial process of esthetic re-ordering that marks the poet's work during this period, is surely one of Baraka's most important poems. In that the work represents the attitude of a generation of emerging black writers, it is even more generally important.

Crow Jane is the muse who hold the poet and his peers in thrall. The primary concern of the poems of *The Dead Lecturer* is the destruction of her pervasive, dehumanizing influence. Her death is prophecied in the epigraph from country bluesman, Mississippi Joe Williams:

> Crow Jane, Crow Jane, don't hold your head so high,
> You realize, baby, you got to lay down and die.

The black woman of Williams's lyric, like little Jim Crow, a figure from minstrelsy, is transformed and, in the process, takes on vastly symbolic proportions. Just as the former name became synonymous with institutionalized *apartheid*, American style, Crow Jane (at least in Baraka's sequence) becomes mythical patroness of the arts as practiced in the American wasteland. Fischer says, in his excellent discussion of the poems of *The Dead Lecturer*, "Crow Jane is the siren who lures the black poet by praising his supposedly Westernized qualities—his intellect, his poetic gift—encouraging him to transform his blackness into the terms of white art."[9] Although Fischer's reading is astute, it would perhaps be more precisely expressed with the substitution of "anti-humanistic" for "white." For, as late as 1963, Baraka could still find praise for certain white writers. In his essay "Black Writing," he speaks of the morality of "white writers like William Burroughs or Edward Dorn (to whom *The Dead Lecturer* is

dedicated) or Hubert Selby [who] show an American as alien to the
fattest enhabitants of this society as any honest black man's emotional history."[10] They somehow managed to escape the blandishments of Crow Jane or "Mama Death," as the poet calls her in the
first poem, "For Crow Jane." In this poem we see her blocking the
natural and virile expression of the now-prostituted poet:

> Wind
> and light, from
> the lady's hand. Cold
> stuff, placed against
> strong man's lips. Young gigolo's
> of the 3rd estate.

The poet goes on to indict her for her sterility also in the first poem.
She is called:

> [. . .] Old lady
> of flaking eyes. Moon lady
> of useless thighs.

The second poem of the sequence, "Crow Jane's Manner," is a
continuation of this attack on the lady and the values she symbolizes. Those elements so frequently condemned in the other works are
treated anew here, particularly deathly analysis, the enemy of action.
Crow Jane and her followers have placed icy reflection on holy
ground and they approach it with religious fervor. Crow Jane's manner:

> Is some pilgrimage
> to thought.

Emphasizing her sterility, the poet calls her:

> Dead Virgin
> of the mind's echo. Dead lady
> of thinking.

The poet laments his failure to withstand the deathly charms of
Crow Jane as well as the failure of his entrapped peers. She has des-

troyed legions. Yet the poet forsees the end of his involvement with
her. He speaks of himself:

> (Me, the last . . . black lip hung
> in dawn's gray wind. The last,
> [. . .]

"Gray," of course, replaced "ofay" as the slang term for *whites* in
the '60's. It is with this slang meaning in mind that we must see the
frequent use of the word throughout *The Dead Lecturer*. It reverber-
ates in the poem "The Invention of Comics," wherein the poet
speaks of his soul and "the menace of its greyness," *i.e.*, its whiteness. In the third poem of the sequence, "Crow Jane in High Society," we see this usage again. First the poet speaks of the lady's
seductive technique. Constantly promoting the rot of reflection, she
looks for:

> Openings
> where she can lay all
> this greasy talk
> on somebody. Me, once. Now
> I am her teller.
>   (And I tell
> her symbols as the grey movement
> of clouds. Leave
> grey movements
> of clouds. Leave, always,
> [. . .]

This is the poet's primary concern at this point. He wants desperately
to leave those sterile literary movements more and more associated
with the general moral failure of white liberalism. This failure, he
feels, is most glaringly present in the literary coterie of which he is a
part. The cloud imagery underscores their separation from real human concerns.

After speaking of the tenacity of her influence and her false
promise in "Crow Jane the Crook," the poet projects her death in
the final poem, "The Dead Lady Canonized." With the putrid artifacts associated with her decadence, the poet wants to:

[. . .] Erect
for that lady, a grave of her own.

The sequence ends with a prayer to Damballah, a deity from "voo-doo" worship, who will be invoked again in "Black Dada Nihilis-mus," the poem that is most logically seen as an outgrowth of "Crow Jane." Damballah, the strong and turbulent serpent god, is asked to abort the future creations conceived by Crow Jane:

[. . .] The lady is dead, may the Gods,
(those others
beg our forgiveness, And Damballah, kind father,
sew up
her bleeding hold.

In "LeRoi Jones Talking," an essay from *Home*, the poet says that the black American should "bring out a little American dada . . . . scream in verse an honest history of America."[11] This is pre-cisely what he does in the poem "Black Dada Nihilismus," a searing example of the poem put to political use. In "Short Speech to My Friends," the poet advised:

Let the combination of Morality
and inhumanity
begin.

"Black Dada Nihilismus" is evidence of his having followed his own advice, for here we see *in extremis* the righteous rage sought in the plaintive lyrics of *Preface*. This kind of commitment is made possible only by the end of the debilitating influence of Crow Jane. In this poem Baraka addresses a new muse, one who is the very antithesis of Crow Jane. This force, like the early art movement for which it is named, is set on demolishing all existing ethical and esthetic stand-ards, especially those standards that keep the two concerns (ethical and esthetic) separate. Here, as in other places, Baraka ironically evinces the pervasiveness of his "Westernism" most glaringly in attempting to reject it. This is particularly evident, for example, in the dramatist's use of German legend in *Dutchman*. This irony is also obvious in "Black Dada," in that the militant black poet invokes a deity named for the rebellious European art movement of the early Twentieth Century. Baraka, of course, realized that his concerns and those of the Dadaists were extremely similar, indeed, identical. Like the Dadaists, he proposes an art that is consciously in revolt against the complacency of convention. He also shares their belief that no attack on smugness can be dismissed as "too extreme." For the Dadaist, the success of a given work was measured largely in terms of its provocative effect on the exemplars of customary behavior. By forcing the public to acknowledge their shocking and irrational creations, the Dadaists hoped to extort from the public a reevaluation and purging of traditional values. Behind this proposition, of course, was the pervasive Dadiast belief that these outmoded traditional values were responsible for the tragedy of the First World War. In Baraka's opinion, his peers and the American public in general exhibited the same "rational" smugness in the face of a latter day evil. He suggests that there should be movers on the American socio-political scene as well as the art scene who are imbued with the same holy iconoclasm that motivated the original Dadaists.

The poem begins with heavy emphasis on the repudiation of old models and beliefs. The tenacity of these evil influences is evidenced in the poet's violently purgative lines. Furthermore, by opening the poem with a period, he seems to tell us that this is the real beginning of his work and that all that preceded it is renounced:

<blockquote>
Against what light

is false what breath
sucked, for deadness.

Murder, the cleansed

purpose, frail, against
God, if they bring him

bleeding, I would not

forgive, or even call him
black dada nihilismus.
</blockquote>

The orderly, parallel structure of these and the remaining lines of the first section, as well as those of the first half of the second section, is effectively contrasted with the markedly agitated appearance of the angry final lines.

After rejecting the God of the West, the poet attacks those who have, under the guise of art, confused the spiritual and the material. Their error is the same as that of the poet's artist friends. He also attacks the assimilationist urge that drains so much of the moral vitality of America:

> The protestant love, wide windows,
> color blocked to Mondrian, and the
> ugly silent deaths of jews under
> the surgeon's knife. (To awake on
> 69th street with money and a hip
> nose.

The Jews of these highly symbolic lines are like the blacks of "Hymn for Lanie Poo." They have gotten rid of all Jewish traits, even to the extent of plastic surgery, getting "hip," i.e., acceptable, noses. In order to thrive in America, they have assimilated, or subjected themselves to "ugly silent deaths." Baraka is even more explicit on this issue in the essay "The Last Days of the American Empire." After speaking of other white ethnic assimilationists, he asks concerning Jewish Americans: "The Jewish Radicals, Socialists, Communists, etc. of the '30's, what happened to them? Have they all disappeared into those sullen suburbs hoping Norman Podhortez or Leslie Fiedler will say something real? The price the immigrant paid to get into America was that they had to become Americans."[12] By this Baraka means that all who assimilate, all who give up selfhood, forfeit their souls. He is, as stated earlier, becoming increasingly convinced that the black American alone does not run this risk. Because of his high visibility (Ralph Ellison's contrary metaphorical implication to the side), the black American cannot easily disappear into the woodwork of America.

The poet ends the first section of this two-part poem with invocations to Hermes, Trismegistus, and Moctezuma. Hermes, the arch shape-shifter of Greek mythology and one of the earliest trickster figures of literature, is invoked for his cunning powers. Hermes Trismegistus, also known as Thoth, the Egyptian god from whom the Greek god derived, was reputed author of the so-called "hermetic" writings, works of relevation on occult subjects and theology. He is said to have been the "patron of all arts dependent on writing."[13] Given the poet's conception of his emerging esthetic posture, we can better understand the invocation to Trismegistus. He concludes with the hope that "dead Moctezuma," a casuality of Western enterprise:

> find the West
>
> a grey hideous space.

The second section opens with sharper focus on the theme of the decadence of the West. We can expect nothing else of value from her drained self-conscious artists:

> From Sartre, a white man, it gave
> the last breath. And we beg him die,
> before he is killed.

The extent to which the poet has begun to associate sterility and anti-humanism not only with the group of wrong-headed poets, but also with whites in general, is seen in some of the most graphic lines the poet ever wrote. He exhorts his imaginary spirit of rebellion:

> [. . .] Come up, black dada
> nihilismis. Rape the white girls. Rape
> their fathers. Cut the mothers' throats.
> Black dada nihilismus, choke my friends
>
> In their bedrooms with their drinks spilling
> and restless for tilting hips or dark liver
> lips sucking splinters from the master's thigh.

Because of the obvious sensationalism, the most important aspect of the quoted lines is generally obscured. Here, above all we see a continuation of the poet's attack on his literary friends. The violence he proposes for them must be seen in symbolic terms. He wants to *choke* them, *i.e.*, cut off their voices, the articulation of their deathly "thought." He says, finally, in the last quoted lines, that he no longer receives sustenance from them, hollow men that they are.

The poet concludes with a final repudiation of his experiences in academia, the "ugliness, learned in the dome" and "colored holy."

He does recall other things taught him by his mentors, however, things that he will use against them. Just as Clay will do in *Dutchman*, the speaker of "Black Dada Nihilismus" tells white America of the danger of his digesting the more brutal facts of Western exploitation. In the voice of the ghetto, he says:

> 'member
> what you said
> money, God, power,
> a moral code, so cruel
> it destroyed Byzantium, Tenochtitlan, Commanch
>
> (got it *Baby!*)

The poet, fully aware of the destructure forces of the Western world, invokes the spirit of retribution in memory of various "victims"—a favorite word of the writer—of these forces. The catalogue of victims includes several black entertainers: Willie Best (who will be more fully discussed later): Buckwheat, of "The Little Rascals" fame: Billie Holiday, the tragic "Lady Day" of song (see Baraka's "The Dark Lady or the Sonnets" in *Black Music*): Mantan Moreland, comedian. The list also includes black freedom fighters W.E.B. DuBois, Toussaint L'Ouverture, Patrice Lumumba, and Denmark Vesey, as well as the poet's maternal grandfather, Tom Russ, to whom *Dutchman* is dedicated.

In spite of the poem's rage, it seems to end on a somber and plaintive note. The poet asks, in conclusion:

> (May a lost god damballah, rest or save us
> against the murders we intend
> against his lost white children
> black dada nihilismus

Damballah, the serpent god referred to in "The Dead Lady Canonized," originally a West African (Yoruba) deity, did not survive the journey to the United States. Hence, he is a lost god, though worshipped by some Haitian voodoo cults. Even in the seemingly mitigating lines of this final prayer, we see the poet's anger at the destruction of non-white cultures and value systems. The key word of these lines is "lost," used twice. The poet sees his job as that of reclamation. He must reclaim a sense of worth and tradition for the victims of the West. He must also work toward the reclamation of a more spiritual world view for a people desperately in need of it.

The tone of "Black Dada . . ." is carried over into "A Contract (for the Destruction and Rebuilding of Paterson," the third poem of *The Dead Lecturer*. The title of this poem would indicate that the early attachment to William Carlos Williams is still operative. A consideration of the content offers even more conclusive proof. There is Williams's concern with the dehumanizing nature of city life and the deterioration of language (and by extension, poetry) in the modern urban setting:

> Flesh, and cars, tar, dug holes beneath stone
> a rude hierarchy of money, band saws cross out
> music, feeling. Even speech, corrodes.
> I came here
> from where I sat boiling in my veins, cold fear
> at the death of men, the death of learning, in
> cold fear, at my own.

The poet shows, by the extreme concreteness of the introductory lines of this poem, that he still attempts to "make a poetry with what [he feels] is useful and can be saved out of all the garbage of our lives" (see note 22, chapter I). Baraka's concern with the tactile is evidence of his sharing the famous Williams dictum "no ideas but in things."

In "A Contract . . ." there is no invocation to an imaginary or symbolic principle of revolution as in "Black Dada. . . ." The poet actually exhorts the victims of the oppressive capitalistic system to seek their own retribution. After chiding the inactivity of abused but "stupid niggers," he talks of the misguided intra-group violence of Puerto Ricans:

> . . . Loud spics kill each other, and will not
>
> make the simple trip to Tiffany's. Will not smash their stainless
> heads, against the simple effrontery of so callous a code as gain.

Although written at least four years before the famous poem "Black People" (used by a judge as evidence of the poet's attempt to incite a

riot), these lines are almost identical to those of the latter work. This
poem closely approximates the later poems also in the poet's momentary exhortation to blacks. It is the only poem of *The Dead Lecturer* that is actually addressed to the black audience, the intended
auditors of all the latter works. Again chiding them for their passive
natures, the poet says:

> You are no brothers, dirty woogies, dying under rinds, in
>   massa's
> droopy tuxedos.

He ends this exhortation by showing, with tongue-in cheek
manner, that he has digested the basic teachings of Marx as well as
some knowledge of Latin. In an effort to prove to the victims that
they are not powerless against the owners of the earth, he speaks of
their own disregarded, through precious, resources. The poor must be
strengthened in the realization that:

> [. . .] even the stupid fruit of their loins is gold or
> something
> else they cannot eat.

The "woogies" and "spics" of these lines are, of course, *proletarians*,
and that word comes from the Latin *proletarius*, which means a person whose sole wealth is his offspring, *i.e., proles*. The poet seems to
say that the poor must show the same dedication in protecting and
sustaining this, the most precious wealth of all, that the owners show
in protecting their more foully begotten riches. Such coded and extremely wry witticisms are the only concessions to humor seen in
the intense poetry of this period. In the later works this concern with
the children becomes an obsession, for one of the poet's most engrossing themes is the assertion of a positive image for future gener-
ations. Note the conclusion to "Black People":

> [. . .] let's get to gather the fruit
> of the sun, let's make a world we want black children to grow and learn
>   in
> do not let your children when they grow look in your face and curse you
>   by
> pitying your tomish ways.

Although most of the poems of this period do not call so

overtly for violent or revolutionary action, evidence of the writer's reorientation is seen in his increasing use of the materials of black life. This is, of course, all a part of the poet's insistence on chronicling "an honest black man's emotional history" in America (see notes 9 and 10). The poignant "Poem for Willie Best" must be considered in this light. Willie Best, a black character actor also known as "Sleep n' Eat," played in numerous Hollywood films of the '30's and '40's. In the tradition of Stepin Fetchit and Mantan Moreland, Willie is best remembered for his patented portrayal of the mythical, shuffling, ghostfearing ("Come on feets, do yo' stuff") black of American movies. Willie's credits include "The Ghost Breakers," "A-Haunting We will Go," a Charlie Chan movie, "The Red Dragon," and many others. The actor died in 1962. This poem, written shortly thereafter, is obviously in memoriam. Stylistically, this work also seems to be a markedly conscious effort on the part of the poet at capturing the essence of the jazz rendition (recall "The Bridge," discussed in Chapter I).

The first section of the poem focuses on the painful double consciousness forced upon the black American. In a society in which his skin is an extreme liability, the black man, in order to survive, often had to resort to role-playing. The roles, generally the kind played by Willie Best and other black buffoons of movie fame, soothed the consciences of many whites, but they exacted a terrible spiritual toll from the black "players" themeselves, who were always aware of their inner or *real* selves. The early poet Paul Lawrence Dunbar expressed the trauma in his oft-anthologized "We Wear The Mask." Baraka's "Poem for Willie Best," written more than a half a century later and in the modern idiom, *suggests* what Dunbar so explicitly *says*. He begins with a description of Willie's screen image:

> The face sings, alone
> at the top
>   of the body. All
> flesh, all song, aligned. For Hell
> is silent, at those cracked lips
> flakes of skin and mind
> twist and whistle softly
> as they fall.

There is the concern with the appearance and the reality of Willie.

The first four lines, with emphasis on physicality and song, exude *performance*. In the remaining lines, however, we see a contrasting concern with the player's anxiety-ridden inner being.

In lines obviously addressed to himself, the poet shows his strong sense of kinship with Willie. They even share a common identity. As he painfully recalls the distorted screen image of the player, the poet tells himself:

>   It was your own death
>   you saw. Your own face, stiff
>   and raw.

The poet, too, is a victim. He sees his specific victimization, however, in the fact that he, like Willie, desires to create in a society in which even his existence is met with antipathy. Willie Best becomes an archetype of thwarted black artistry. In his death we see imaged the tragic plight of black creative genius in America. Some of these characters were catalogued in "Black Dada. . . ." Others, Charlie Parker and Bessie Smith, are cited in *Dutchman*. These creators, as well as the poet, were prey to the same destructive forces responsible for Willie's end.

>   [. . .] His blood, for a time
>   alive, and huddled in a door
>   way, struggling to sing. Rain
>   washes it into cracks. Pits
>   whose bottoms are famous. Whose sides
>   are innocent broadcasts
>   of another life.

The second section continues the treatment of the themes of double consciousness and thwarted black artistry, both expressed with the highly suggestive imagery of crucifixion. Again the poet emphasizes the murderous suppression of the black creator's spirit. There is no audience in America for the black artist, or black American in general, who would release his true feelings. Black performance, American style, means:

>   the man, and his material, driven in
>   the ground. If the head rolls back

and the mouth opens, screamed into
existence, there will be perhaps
only the slightest hint of movement
a smear; no help will come. No one
will turn to that station again.

The third section of this work is concerned with the burden of
the racial past and its relation to the crucial present (early 1960's)
moment in the black American's existence. Willie Best and the race
of which he is symbol have been divested of their racial heritage.
They are, moreover, unprotected from the destroying or, perhaps,
bleaching elements of a hostile society.

At a cross roads, sits the
player. No drum, no umbrella, even
though it's raining.

In the rapid-fire manner of the cinema, the poet gives us images of
the racial past, images that are simultaneously representative of painful deprivation and the intense instinct for survival.

5 lb neckbones.
5 lb hog innards
10 bottles cheap wine.

There are, on the other hand, images of the anguish and suffering put
upon the black American in the name of Christianity, "300 men on
horseback/75 bibles." These lines recall the fierce repudiation of
religiosity in "Black Dada. . . ." Indeed, the hypocrisy of the "godly"
leads the poet to this scathing renunciation. He says of "God":

[. . .] if they bring him
bleeding, I would not
forgive, or even call him
black dada nihilismus.

After a brief lament for the player (section four), the poet
considers the exuberance of black creativity. In so doing he subtly
returns to the attack on his literary peers and their overly reflective
pursuits. Here the poet effectively invokes images from the black

minstrel tradition, to which Willie Best belonged. He suggests that
art must be expressive, in the manner of black dance. It must transcend cold cerebration:

> This is the dance of the raised
> leg. Of the hand on the knee
> quickly.
>   As a dance it punishes
> speech.

Black music, as stated earlier, is another model for the poet in search
of a new mode of expression. It, too, has "unspeakable" expressive
powers:

> This is the song
> of the highest C.
>   The falsetto. An elegance
> that punishes silence.

"Poem for Willie Best" ends in a manner reminiscent of the
traditional jazz rendition. In the final section, there is a marked return to the thematic issues of the first. The effect is quite like that
produced by the jazz musician's return to the "head" after his more
imaginative improvised statement. The extremely difficult and "private" penultimate section, like the most daring of improvisations,
makes the final section even more plausibly a restatement of the
theme. Once again the theme of double consciousness is explicity referred to. Willie Best (and the black American) is in actuality:

> A renegade
> behind the mask. And
> even the mask, a renegade
> disguise.

He has many masks. The masks, all of which coincide with some consoling stereotype in the mind of the dominant culture, are varied:

> Lazy
> Frightened
> Thieving
> Very potent sexually

Scars
Generally inferior
(but natural
rhythms.

The poet knows that the conception of Willie held by white America is not a valid one, however:

It is an obscene invention.
A white sticky discharge.

Section one is recalled also in the reference to the "huddled blood" of Willie Best and all black creators. As in section three, the poet re-emphasizes the crucial nature of the times for the black American.

And he sits
wet at the crossroads, remembering distinctly
each weightless face that eases by. (Sun at
the back door, and that hideous mindless grin.
(Hear?

Evidence of the poet's increasing usage of the historical theme is seen throughout the works of *Sabotage*, most notably in the first poem of that collection, "Three Modes of History and Culture." In the sweeping lines of this poem we see vivid images of the so-called "great migration," the movement of southern rural blacks to the urban centers of the North. The same empathy and sense of self-discovery that marked the historical passages of "Poem for Willie Best" are evident in "Three Modes. . . ." He starts with the experience of slavery and moves to the more subtle dehumanization of the modern factory:

From heavy beginnings. Plantations,
learning
America, as speech, and a common emptiness. Songs knocking
Inside old women's faces. Knocking through cardboard trunks.
Trains
leaning north, catching hellfire in windows, passing through
the first ignoble cities of missouri, to illinois, and the panting
Chicago.
And then all ways, we go where flesh is cheap. Where factories
sit open, burning the chiefs. Make your way! Up through fog and
history [. . .]

It is this heightened sense of the desperate entrapment of the black American that accounts for the growing sense of mission or prophecy in the poems of this period. He tells himself in "Citizen Cane":

> Roi, finish this poem, someone's about to need you. Roi,
> dial the mystic number, ask for holy beads, directions,
> plans for the destruction of New York. . . .
> Get up and hit
> someone, like you useta. Don't sit here trembling under the
> hammer.

The urgency of the moment cannot be denied, and all who turn from the demands of the times are guilty of treason. The poet's personal sense of guilt, so overwhelmingly present in *Preface*, returns, but with more directly racial meaning. He suffers from the feeling that his art has been of no real use to those most desperately in need of him. His most piercing anguish stems from the feeling that he has been lured from his sources. Again the censure falls on the friends. He says in "The People Burning, *May-Day! May-Day!*" a poem which expresses the urgency of the moment in title alone:

> Now they ask me to be a jew or italian, and turn from the moment
> disappearing into the clock of treasonable safety, like reruns
> of films, with sacred coon stars. . . .
> Forget your whole life, pop your fingers in a closed room,
> hopped-up witch doctor for the cowards of a recent generation. It is
> choice, now, like a philosophy problem. It is choice, now, and
> the weight is specific and personal [. . .]

Again, the poet identifies with Willie Best, Stepin Fetchit, and Mantan Moreland. Like them ("sacred coon stars"), he has assumed a role of self-denial. It is, however, a role that the poet can no longer play. He says, moreover, in lines that seem to post-date the successes of the angry dramatic productions, that he will no longer be content to exorcise the collective guilt of liberal America.

The poet senses that his first task of ordering lies in the ending of his particular burden of double consciousness. He must either stop writing altogether and concentrate on his new socio-political aims, or he can work more vigorously toward effecting a rapproachment between his art and his activism. He opts for the latter. We are forewarned in "Rhythm and Blues (1 (for Robert Williams in exile)" of the poetry to come. Like Afro-American musical expression, Baraka's exuberant, teaching verse will be comprised of "The roaring harmonies of need." In what amounts to a farewell to the Village coterie, the poet says:

> I am deaf and blind and lost and will not again sing your quiet
> verse. I have lost
> even the act of poetry, and writhe now for cool horizonless dawn.
> The
> shake and chant, bulled electric motion, figure of what will
> be
> as it sits beside me waiting to live past my own meekness . . .
> There will be those
> who will tell you it will be beautiful.

Despite the significant revisions and departures in the poet's world-view, the technique of Baraka's poetry does not change drastically at this stage of his career. Those attributes discussed in the first chapter are still in evidence. The flexibility of form and employment of speech rhythm are still there. However, the frequent discontinuities and syntactic difficulties are increasingly juxtaposed with lines of searing clarity. The last quoted lines are exemplary of this tendency toward prosaic statement. If anything, the contrasting nature of the lines underscores the schizoid state of the poet, who writes, in one passage, the cryptic verse demanded by his *avant garde* peers and, in the next, the direct lines more typical of the *Umbra* poets. Although the poet will continue in his efforts to resolve this basic conflict, even the latter works, *i.e.*, those supposedly written for the edification of the black masses, frequently are as inaccessible or private as any written for the Village coterie.

There are still other minor changes in the verse just considered. As noted before, these poems, generally speaking, are not characterized by the wry humor (what I called "blues" humor in Chapter I— see page *14*) so pervasive in *Preface*. The poet discards even the therapeutic effect of laughter-in-despair in the taut, angry lines of his "middle passage." Although this concession may be, on first glance, attributed to the author's sparing use of popular culture images, a more thorough study shows that the latter poems are also characterized by frequent allusion to such images. In the latter poems, however, Superman, the Lone Ranger, the Shadow, Nick Charles, and others are supplanted by the victimized "sacred coon stars" of movie fame. This shift in images brings about a completely different tone in the verse. On the one hand we get wry humor, on the other, sheer pathos. There are other such transformations of image patterns in the poems of *The Dead Lecturer* and *Sabotage*. The poet's changing use of the imagery of the city is one of the more striking examples. In the poems of *Preface*, the "long empty streets," bridges, subway rails, busses, and church bells all reinforce the poet's sense of alienation and despair. When used in the poems of *The Dead Lecturer* the imagery of the city bears a less personal burden. The reader must focus on the harsh reality of ghetto life. Neither the poems of *The Dead Lecturer* or *Sabotage* evince the lush natural imagery of "Hymn for Lanie Poo" or "The Clearing." Baraka himself seems to bid farewell to such poetry in the recollective lyric "This In the Clearing I Once Spoke of."

Baraka, at this juncture, also seems to be even more inventive regarding the visual effect of the poems. In most cases appearance and content are effectively yoked. The tight, vertical configurations of *The Dead Lecturer* somehow manage to reinforce our appreciation of the self-involvement so abhorred in these very lyrics. Other works employ the long line to good effect. The previously mentioned "Three Modes . . ." is a striking example. "Gatsby's Theory of Assthetics" *looks* like anything *but* the traditional poem. It bears little resemblance to even the most experimental poem. Comprised of six "paragraphs," it appears to be a prose essay. This is precisely the appearance, or "form," that Baraka wanted. With "Gatsby's Theory . . ." the poet wants to force the reader into a reconsideration of his preconceived notions concerning the art of poetry. The poem begins:

> Verse, as a form, is artificial. Poetry is not a form, but rather
> a result. Whatever the matter, its meaning, if precise enough
> in its information (and direction) of the world, is poetic. The
> poetic is the value of poetry, and any concatenation of elements
> is sufficient to induce the poetic. . . .

This poem, by nature of its configuration and content, seems to show us that the poet has not swerved, at least technically speaking, from the ideals espoused in Don Allen's *New American Poetry 1945-1960* (see note 22, first chapter). There have been remarkable thematic changes, however. Like the poems, the plays from this phase of the writer's career manifest these changes.

Dutchman and *The Slave*

    Dutchman and *The Slave*, Baraka's most popular and commercially successful plays, can be interpreted as dramatizations of the intense personal conflict seen in the poetry of this period. Both are fundamentally concerned with the author's intense conviction that the black American is the last moral voice, *i.e.*, the last outsider or objective seer, in a corrupt land. As such, both plays address themselves to the hazards inherent in the black man's desire to meld into the oppressive structure of America. In these works the central figure of the homosexual as outsider or as Beatnik is replaced by the schizoid black poet. Like the homosexuals of the early plays, the protagonists of *Dutchman* and *The Slave* reflect the particular psycho-social situation of the poet. Both Clay and Walker Vessesls resemble LeRoi Jones himself or young Ray of *The Toilet*, now grown up. They are middle class black poets who, in varying degrees, articulate disillusionment with their assimilationist lifestyles. Clay, in opposition to his deepest desires, chooses a life of self-denial and is killed. Walker, however, through the most violent of means, attempts to assert his identity and simultaneously performs the vital function of exorcism for his guilt-ridden creator. Of course, the plays transcend esoteric and private meaning. This is evident in the general acclaim accorded *Dutchman*, the writer's best known dramatic work. Moreover, although *The Slave* is definitely not the artistic equal of *Dutchman*, it, too, deserves more than passing consideration.

    In his treatment of *The Baptism*, Donald Costello, we recall, says, "Jones strains to be shocking; and the play ends up to be incoherent and adolescent, with scatter-shot fury."[14] Although this is a harsh judgment, Costello's reaction is understandable in light of the general lack of restraint in this early effort. Evidence of Baraka's growth as a dramatist is seen in the extreme unlikelihood of even the most hostile of critics ever referring to the "scatter-shot fury" of *Dutchman*. This play definitely finds its mark, and this is due in large part to the author's skillful and economic employment of basic dramatic conventions and a masterful sense of rhythm.

Like the train of its setting, *Dutchman* moves with tremendous bursts of energy and periodic lulls. As the train pulls out of the station, the tension accelerates immediately with Lula's increasingly abusive treatment of Clay, who, by virtue of his apparent naivete, wins the sympathy of the audience. Midway through the play, however, this incessant goading threatens to completely exasperate the audience, to drain them all too hastily. The maturing dramatist effectively counters this by ending the first scene. By dividing the action into two scenes, he not only gives the audience a chance to regroup emotionally, he also manages to give the play a greater sense of depth. After those few seconds of darkness, the audience views the opening action of scene II with the distinct feeling that a great deal has happened, as well as the hope that Clay has started to better acquit himself with Lena. This hope is short-lived, however, for the dramatist starts anew the pattern of scene I as the train pulls out at the beginning of scene II.

Again Lula takes the initiative. She tells Clay how they will behave at the party, utters more strange statements of the kind that kept him off-balance throughout the first scene, and finally attacks him with an intensity surpassing that of the first scene. Like the screaming train, the action of the play is near peak acceleration. At this point, *i.e.*, during Lula's most vile outpouring, both Clay and his sympathetic viewers are thoroughly exhausted and provoked. Clay's outburst, a masterful rendering of the age-old dramatic reversal, even goes beyond the earlier break in action in that it simultaneously relieves and maintains tension. It relieves the tension inasmuch as it fulfills our desire for some self-assertion on Clay's part. Yet it maintains tension in the promise of a final and violent clash of antagonistic forces. Although we are ready for the expected clash, Baraka puts us off guard with his fine sense of timing. He lulls us into forgetting the promised end with the calm immediately following Clay's eruption. Consequently, we rest in the feeling that Lula has finally been silenced. At this point, we are hit with the final and even more shattering reversal in Clay's murder.

The train and the action of *Dutchman* simultaneously grind to a halt. However, in the troubling denouement, we perceive evidence of the entire pattern beginning anew with the entrance of the anonymous young man, who is, from all appearance, like Clay or Warren Enright, a "well-known type." As the train accelerates, this young man's tragic end is inevitably projected in our minds.

Along with his masterful manipulation of suspense and tension, Baraka shows his growth in the ease with which he combines the mythic and the literal in *Dutchman*. We are prepared for his duality of meaning from the opening lines of the text. *Dutchman* takes place *"In the flying underbelly of the city. Steaming hot, and summer on top, outside. Underground. The subway heaped in modern myth."* The setting suggests that the play will delve into the troubling, but too often denied truths of race relations, American style. This setting, like the encounter between the exaggeratedly "real" characters, is, indeed, meant to represent a more elusive inner or psychic reality. As if he wanted to make sure no one mistook this work for the overt naturalism of, say, *The Toilet*, Baraka gives important alternative directions: *"Dimlights and darkness whistling by against the glass. (Or paste the lights, as admitted props right on the subway windows."* He seeks to snythesize the naturalistic and expressionistic modes, to take the best each has to offer. This is evidenced not only in his approach to setting, but also in the characterization of *Dutchman*. Lula and Clay are simultaneously "real" persons and highly symbolic types. The powerful effect of the drama, derived from this synthesis of artistic modes, has been compared frequently to that of Albee's *The Zoo Story*, another lean, parable-like work concerned wtih the tragic consequences of failure to communicate.

The play's title and setting have prompted many commentators to explore its mythic implications. Hugh Nelson asserts, rather convincingly, that Baraka converts the legend of "the Flying Dutchman" into modern myth. Seeing Lula as the doomed Dutchman and Clay as the pure lover who could release her from her deathly existence, Nelson notes striking similarities in the legendary ship and Baraka's train. The cold, impersonal train, like the doomed ship,

seems to operate "according to some diabolical plan. It goes nowhere, never emerges from its darkness; reaching one terminus, it
reverses itself and speeds back towards the other with brief pauses at
identical stations. . . ."[15] Like the crew of the "Dutchman," Baraka's passengers exhibit the same spiritual torpor in acceding to the
wishes of their "captain," Lula. Other commentators have noted the
implication of the myth of Adam and Eve—and on occasion, Lilith—
in the story of Clay and Lula. It is obvious that Baraka drew upon all
these elements in the creation of *Dutchman.*

We notice, first, by the dedicatory inscription of the text
Dutchman and The Slave that both plays are products of the poet's
"middle passage." The plays are dedicated to the author's maternal
grandparents, "Thomas Everett Russ, American pioneer, and Anna
Cherry Brock Russ." This is the same "Tom Russ" catalogued along
with the victimized heroes of the concluding lines of "Black Dada. . . ." In this dedication, the dramatist announces the theme of
Dutchman, i.e., the search for usable black roots or the moral
strength and authenticity of the racial past. By virtue of the dedicatory inscription, the dramatist embraces all that Clay denies.

Like the poems of *The Dead Lecturer* and *Sabotage, Dutchman* is concerned with the vigorous and non-apologetic assertion of
the author's racial and emotional attachments and aimed at the
eradication of the assimilationist syndrome. This purpose is explicitly spelled out in "Death Is Not as Natural as You Fags Seem to
Think," a poem from *Sabotage.* The poet warns the Clays of the
world:

> I hunt
> the black puritan
>   (Half-screamer
> in dull tones
> of another forest.
>
> Respecter of power.

Baraka emphasizes the schizoid nature of the black middle-class with
the phrase "black puritan." For the dramatist, who believes that
black life *is* essentially characterized by an unihibited earthiness, this

is a self-contradictory perversion. Clay is, moreover, a "half-scream-er" because he manages to keep his primeval, uninhibited self, as well as his justified rage, so well in check. E. Franklin Frazier, whose work profoundly affected Baraka during this phase of the artist's career, specifically mentions the repressed violence of the black middle class. He says in *Black Bourgeoisie:*

> Middle-class Negroes do not express their resentment against discrim-inations and insults in violent outbreaks, as lowerclass Negroes often do. They constantly repress their hositility toward whites and seek to soothe their hurt self-esteem in all kinds of rationalizations.... Even middle-class Negroes who gain a reputation for exhibiting "objectiv-ity" and a "statesmanlike" attitude on racial discrimination harbor deep-seated hostilities toward whites. A Negro college president who has been considered such an interracial "statesman" once confessed to the writer that some day he was going to "break loose" and tell white people what he really thought. However, it is unlikely that a middle-class Negro of his standing will ever "break loose."[16]

Unlikely though it may be, Clay, Baraka's representative of the black middle class, finally does break loose, and his vitriolic response is a measure of his long-repressed inner turmoil. Like Willie Best and the other black "performers" who appear in the works of this phase of Baraka's career, even Clay is tired of the burden of double conscious-ness, the weight of the mask.

As his name implies, Clay is the black American who allows himself to be molded into the image of white middle-class society. Like Ray of *The Toilet*, he is a son of the black middle class. He is also a graduate of a college quite like "Capstone U." of "The Alter-native" (*Tales*). Lula is close to the truth when she tells Clay that he "went to a colored college where everybody thought they were Aver-ell Harriman." Clay's every act is designed to distance him from the reality of black existence in America. This self-denial is most power-fully imaged in his ardent anticipation of the party and his dream of complete possession of Lula. He has dedicated himself to the pursuit of her and all that she symbolizes. Baraka makes it clear that Clay's tragedy lies in his all-consuming desire to be "involved" with Lula, who is, according to the author, the "spirit of America."

In Lula's flirtation with Clay we see symbolic treatment of the spiritual and moral bankruptcy of the dominant culture. She seeks no real emotional attachment with Clay because she is incapable of the demands of such a relationship. At best, she wants a quick, masturbatory affair. Evidence of Clay's having given himself up to Lula's perverse use is symbolically rendered in his ivy league attire, his reading material, his embryonic bohemian style, and his artistic pursuits, all of which are meant to please the Lulas of the world. His suppliant attitude is evident also in his demeanor in her presence. Lula is clearly in control of the situation from the start, and Clay is content to follow her lead in the repartee.

LULA: Now you say to me, "Lula, Lula, why don't you go to this party with me tonight?" It's your turn, and let those be your lines.

CLAY: Lula, why don't you go to this party with me tonight, Huh?

LULA: Say my name twice before you ask, and no huh's.

CLAY: Lula, Lula, why don't you go to this party with me tonight?

LULA: I'd like to go, Clay, but how can you ask me to go when you barely know me?

CLAY: This is strange, isn't it?

LULA: What kind of reaction is that? You're supposed to say, "Aw come on, we'll get to know each other better at the party."

Just as Lula controls the terms and degree of Clay's "involvement" with her, white America decides on the extent of acceptance accorded the black assimilationist, whose most fervent wish lies in facilitating this grudging acceptance.

Clay's rather pretentious literary concerns are also best understood in terms of his assimilationist dream. He admits that he once thought he was Baudelaire and still facies himself a "would-be poet." His artistic involvement, however, like his whole life, is a sham. Baraka explains the meaning of the black middle-class writer's literary

pursuits in his essay "The Myth of a Negro Literature." His statement is particularly relevant in the case of Clay:

> Literature, for the Negro writer, was always an example of "culture."
> Not in the sense of the more impressive philosophical characteristics of
> a particular social group, but in the narrow sense of "cultivation" or
> "sophistication" by an individual within that group. . . . To be a writer
> was to be "cultivated" in the stunted bourgeois sense of the word. It
> was also to be a "quality" black man. It had nothing to do with the
> investigation of the human soul. It was, and is, a social preoccupation
> rather than an esthetic one.[17]

Clay, then, "would-be poet" and graduate of one of "those ineffect-
ual philanthropies," most assuredly approaches art in this sterile
manner. Much of the guilt of the earlier poems, perhaps, stems from
Baraka's feeling that he had yielded to the same temptation.

Like Clay, Lula is an extremely "real" character. At the same
time, she, too, bears tremendous symbolic weight. The author's
self-contradictory denial of the characters' symbolic meaning only
convinces us of the correctness of the symbolic reading. In answer to
those who found Lula unrealistically "neurotic," Baraka says:

> . . . if she must be symbolic in the way demented academicians use the
> term, she does not exist all all. She is not meant to be a symbol—nor is
> Clay—but a real thing, in a real world. She does not represent any thing
> she is one. And perhaps that thing is America or at least its spirit. You
> remember America, don't you, where they have unsolved murders hap-
> pening before your eyes on television. How crazy, extreme, neurotic,
> does that sound? Lula, for all her alleged insanity, just barely reflects
> the insanity of this hideous place.[18]

Lula, then, is as much a symbol as is Crow Jane (discussed on pages
54-57.) She is, in fact, another verison of Crow Jane, who embodies
the sterile esthetic principles now rejected by the poet. Baraka goes
to great lengths to show us how similar in demeanor these two bitch
goddesses are. Crow Jane:

                    (Wipes
          her nose
          on the draperies. Spills drinks

fondles another man's
life.

Compare her actions to those of Lula, eternal temptress (apples in hand) and possessor of an equally lustful and slovenly manner. We see her *"Wrapping the apple core in a Kleenex and dropping it on the floor"* and *"Putting her hand on Clay's closest knee, drawing it from the knee up to the thigh's hinge. . . ."* Moreover, the sterility of Lula is imaged in a manner recalling that of Crow Jane. Crow Jane's "flaking eyes and useless thighs" are seen in Lula's brittle hand, which by her own admission is as "dry as ashes." Lula is, like Crow Jane, an emasculating "luller." She lulls the young black protagonist from truth and into a life of sham and self-denial.

Lula is a stand-in for the much-maligned peers of *The Dead Lecturer*, those knowledgeable, "arty" ones who hide behind the facade of liberalism of even radical chic but who in actuality prove themselves enemies of real change. Just as the author hunts the "black puritan," he also hunts the Lulas of the world, those liberal "talkers" who rival even the enraged persona of "Black Dada . . ." in revolutionary rhetoric. Lula, like the angry essayist/poet of this phase, literally tells Clay to bring out "a little American dada." Recall her exhortation:

> . . . Christ, God. Get up and scream shit at these people. Like scream meaningless shit in their hopeless faces. Red trains cough Jewish underwear for keeps! Expanding smells of silence. Gravy snot whistling like sea birds. Clay, Clay, you got to break out. Don't sit there dying the way they want you to die. Get up.

In her words we perceive what *appears* to be a genuine hatred for Clay's meek, accommodating existence. There is just enough substance in the "statement" to give an aura of authentic humanistic concern. This is evident in the cryptic allusion to the holocaust, that tragic and exemplary occurence referred to so frequently in Baraka's writings of this period. However, we see, upon close analysis of Lula's words, that she has, in actuality, said nothing. Her words, like the best of liberal cliches, exude humanism but prove to be more empty babble when tested by the demands of the real world.

Lula proves by her vicious response to Clay's long-overdue self-assertion that the last thing she wants him to manifest is self-knowledge. At best, she wants him to exchange one role for a more thoroughly degrading one, that of the super-masculine menial or sexual athlete. By reversing the sterotype of the white-woman-raped-by-bestial-black, Baraka emphasizes his principal assertion that the real perversion and animalism reside with the insensitive dominant culture. Lula's murderous action is all the more meaningful when we consider that she represents what is supposedly the more enlightened segment of the society, *i.e.*, the moral leadership. This aspect is profoundly underscored by the mindlessly obedient, zombie-like action of the other riders of the train, both black and white.

The earlier plays, *The Baptism* and *The Toilet*, were characterized by the dominance of action. Dancing, mock athletic contests, fights (fantasized and real), and mass slaughter all produce an overwhelming sense of movement. Much of the power of *Dutchman*, however, stems from the author's powerful use of language. Detractors of the work frequently assert that the author asks too much of language; *i.e.*, language alone cannot sustain a dramatic production. These critics, however, grossly undervalue not only the tremendously cathartic effect of Baraka's handling of tension but the suggestive gestures of the actors as well. In fact, we are prepared for Lula's neurotic final act by the implications of her earliest gestures. Her actions are subtly fraught with ambiguities. Early on we see her *"Laughing and cutting it off abruptly," "uncrossing and recrossing her legs"*; at another point, she is *"Mock serious, then she howls with laughter."* These gestures, like Clay's many manifestations of discomfort in his role, are of extreme importance and should not be underestimated in any analysis of the play's "action." Nevertheless, *Dutchman* is largely a triumph of language. Although we saw evidence of his sensitivity to the dramatic employment of language in both *The Baptism* and *The Toilet*, *Dutchman* is the apotheosis of this aspect of the author's dramatic work, and it is seen to best advantage in Clay's blistering excoriation.

Throughout most of the play, Clay, entrenched in his role, exhibits only the best behavior and speaks the most respectable English. In fact, about the only grim humor to be seen in this work is that provoked by Clay's squeamishness at Lula's earthy and sexually suggestive comments. Prior to Clay's outburst, the only "profanity"

he utters appears in his weak attempt to be learnedly humorous.
However, just as the exaggeratedly "profane" idiom was right for the
exorcism of sham sanctity in *The Baptism*, the brutal and naked
street idiom is appropriate and most effective in the uncloaking of
racial truths. Clay's linguistic fusillade begins with the command:

> Oh, sit the fuck down.

As he warms to the task, he scathingly attacks her hip bohemianism.

> You great liberated whore! You fuck some black man, and right away
> you're an expert on black people. What a lotta shit that is. The only
> thing you know is that you come if he bangs you hard enough. And
> that's all. The belly rub? You wanted to do the belly rub? Shit, you
> don't even know how. You don't know how. That ol' dipty-dip shit you
> do, rolling your ass like an elephant. Belly rub is not Queens. Belly rub is
> dark places, with big hats and overcoats held up with one arm. Belly
> rub hates you [. . .] Old bald-headed four-eyed ofays popping their
> fingers . . . and don't know yet what they're doing.

Clay continues with his intensely personal and now-famous
reading of black artistry. Bessie Smith's music enabled her to contain
her rage.

> And you don't even understand that Bessie Smith is saying, "Kiss my ass,
> kiss my black unruly ass."

Likewise with Charlie Parker, who was deified by liberated bohemian types:

> Charlie Parker? Charlie Parker. All the hip white boys scream for Bird
> [. . .] would've played not a note of music if he just walked up East
> Sixty-seventh Street and killed the first ten white people he saw. Not
> a note!

Finally he gets around to the exposure of his own artistry as black
middle-class writer:

> And I'm the great would-be poet. Yes. That's right! Poet. Some kind of
> bastard literature . . . All it needs is a simple knife thrust. Just let me
> bleed you whore, and one poem vanished.

Again we see the poet undermining the importance of literary pursuits. Poetry as practiced by himself and his peers is a meaningless luxury, a reflective hindrance in a world dying from the need of positive and direct expression ("need of the simple striking arm. . . ." —"Black Dada . . ."). It is important to note also that the music of Parker and Smith, though indicted for its evasiveness, escapes the stigma attached to the poetry written by Clay. As Baraka has repeatedly stated, Afro-American music reflects the "legitimate emotional resources of the soul in the world." Clay, then, condemns his own poems ("some kind of bastard literature") because they are twice removed from reality. It is significant that Clay, in rejecting the murders and violence that would make him and all blacks "sane," decides to be ". . . a fool. Insane. Safe with my words, and no death, and clean hard thoughts." Again *Words* are inimical to *action*.

Clay's tragic choice—words over action—is evidence of the continuing appeal of Lula. In his final remarks, we sense that he still wants to be involved with her in spite of his brief revolt. It is Clay, not Lula, who mentions the aborted plans for the party, and although he sneeringly reminds her of it:

> Looks like we won't be acting out that little pageant you outlined before, ...

we get the distinct impression that Clay still pants for an affirmative response. He is more than ready to return to life as before. He is still very much bound to Lula and the life she symbolizes. It is this allegiance that causes Clay's death, not the self-assertive outburst. For, during his momentary rage, Clay was most alive and impervious to death. He is killed when he bends across Lula to pick up his books, *i.e.*, to resume the role.

The play ends with the assurance that this tragedy will be repeated. After Clay's murder and the disposal of his body, we observe the concluding action of *Dutchman*.

> *A young Negro of about twenty comes into the coach, with a couple of books under his arm. He sits a few seats in back of LULA. When he is seated she turns and gives him a long slow look. He looks up from his book and drops his book on his lap. Then an old Negro conductor comes into the car, doing a sort of restrained soft shoe, and half*

mumbling the words of some song. He looks at the young man, briefly
with a quick greeting.

CONDUCTOR: Hey brother!

YOUNG MAN: Hey.

(The conductor continues down the aisle with his little dance and the
mumbled song. LULA turns to stare at him and follows his movements
down the aisle. The conductor tips his hat when he reaches her seat,
and continues out the car.)

We see in the young man's recognition of the conductor a tragic acknowledgement of brotherhood. Just as the conductor performs his
soft shoe for Lula's approval, this young man, bearing books, will go
through his own act. In his willingness to continue his performance,
in the manner of Clay, we see the seeds of his death. Baraka concludes that black survival in America can be effected only with the
black man's rejection of the self-denying role assigned by America.
Walker Vessels, the protagonist of *The Slave*, attempts this through-
going rejection.

The Slave: A Fable in a Prologue and Two Acts

Just as "Black Dada. . ." is best explained as an outgrowth of
the "Crow Jane" poems, *The Slave*, is most meaningfully construed
as a companion piece to *Dutchman*. The dramatist himself underlines
the complementary nature of the two works by publishing them
jointly. Walker, like Clay, has been the aspiring black poet. He, too,
has been bound to the ivory tower esthetics of Crow Jane, but he
manages to "break loose," to reject the values of his tutors, while
Clay chooses to sublimate his rage and perpetuate the consoling lies.
Nevertheless, they are brothers, and their basic kinship is seen in
their names. Walker's name, like all the names in these two plays, is
fraught with symbolic implications. On first glance, "Walker Vessels"
seems to suggest the direction and potency so lacking in the easily-
molded and limp implications of "Clay". Such a meaning would per-

haps be plausible were it not for the contradictory evidence of the play. Although Walker has made definite progress along the path to self-definition, he continues to manifest the psychic division of Clay and the poet of *The Dead Lecturer*. So, instead of reading potency and direction into "Walker Vessels," we are closer to the truth of his nature if we see the name in terms of search and fulfillment. On the one hand, he is the untiring seeker of self. On the other, he is the empty receptacle into which a thoroughly committed and revolutionary black consciousness must be poured. Finally, Clay and Walker are similar in that their attachments to the dominant culture are symbolized in their relationships with white women. In both works, the resolution of the problem of dual consciousness in rendered in climactic, tragic confrontations between the poets and the women who personify the dominant culture.

At the end of the first scene of *Dutchman*, Lula entices Clay with the following illusory words:

> [. . .] we'll pretend the people cannot see you. That is, the citizens. And that you are fee of your history. And I am free of my history . . . .
>
>   . . . .

As seen in the subject matter of the poems of this phase, Baraka is becoming increasingly convinced that no American, black or white, is free of his history. The poems evince the growing conviction that a positive self-concept rests upon complete acceptance and understanding of the racial past. The "Prologue" of *The Slave* is a restatement of this conviction.

In the "Prologue" we see Walker *"dressed as an old field slave, balding, with white hair, and an old ragged vest."* In Act I, however, we see this same slave metamorphosed into the 20th Century revolutionary. The revolutionary, a product of his past, literally grows out of the slave. The old slave of the "Prologue" speaks of the insatiable quest for identity and the traditionally consoling lies of the mask, both pervasive issues in the previously-considered works:

> Whatever the core of our lives. What ever the deceit. We live where we are, and seek nothing but ourselves. . . . I am much older than I look . . . or maybe much younger. Whatever I am or seem . . . (*significant*

pause) to you, then let that rest. But figure, still, that you might be lying . . . to save yourself.

This message is underscored by the very style and wording of the "Prologue" itself. The speaker, who *looks* and *acts* the part of "an old field slave," *speaks* in a manner befitting an existentialist philosopher or Beat poet. C. W. E. Bigsby misses the point in dismissing the "Prologue" as "ponderous pretension."[19] Moreover, in the extremely private manner of his delivery, the slave seems to be, like the revolutionary Walker, a surrogate for his creator. The dramatist who was slave to the esthetes and their cryptic and inbred manner will soon be no more. This persona, too, will go the way of the dead lecturer.

Like the poems of *The Dead Lecturer*, the "Prologue" is concerned with moral failure and the drastic need for a reappraisal of values. The old slave addresses his audience, presumably liberals, in much the same way the poet repeatedly addressed his peers. He attacks their smugness as:

A stupid longing not to know . . . which is automatically fulfilled. Automatically triumphs. Automatically makes us killers or foot-dragging celebrities at the core of any filth. And it is a deadly filth that pauses as whatever thing we feel is too righteous to question, too deeply felt to deny.

The old slave exhorts his audience to change, which is the proposition to which Walker, the revolutionary, addresses his life. The play itself seems to be Baraka's first effort in the unabashedly didactic play, what he calls "the revolutionary theatre," described in the following manner:

The Revolutionary Theatre should force change; it should be change. (All their faces turned into the lights and you work on them black nigger magic, and cleanse them at having seen the ugliness. And if the beautiful see themselves, they will love themselves.)

We must make an art that will function so as to call down the actual wrath of world spirit. We are witch doctors and assassins, but we will open a place for the true scientists to expand our consciousness. This is a theatre of assault. The play that will split the heavens for us will be called THE DESTRUCTION OF AMERICA.[20]

It is interesting to compare Baraka's dramatic theory to that of Bertolt Brecht, the 20th Century's most renowned advocate of a political theatre. In Brecht's estimation, the highest form of theatre was that which "awakens [the spectator's] capacity to act"[21] and that which "demands decisions from him."[22] However, Brecht felt it necessary to emphasize the apartness of the theatrical process (The most desirable political theatre always "makes the spectator an observer.")[23] Brecht felt that too much emotional involvement of the part of the viewers sapped them of the energies needed to bring about change in the real world. The viewers should leave the theatre armed with the cool tools of heightened scientific perception. However, Baraka strains for complete emotional involvement on the part of his audience. This becomes most noticeable in his later agit-prop works, some of which depend on ritualistic audience participation. This will be discussed at greater length in the next chapter.

Walker Vessels is a latter-day Denmark Vesey, the figure remembered for leading an aborted slave rebellion in Charleston, South Carolina, and catalogued in "Black Dada. . . ." Before he is able to positively lead his forces, however, Walker must rid his mind of what he sees as the debilitating influence of Western thought. Walker, the would-be liberator, is beset with the problem of his psychological bondage to the Clay syndrome. In spite of the constant reminders of the physical violence surrounding the Easley apartment, the major dramatic interest lies in the painful genesis of Walker's spiritual liberation. In fact, despite the presence of three actors on stage, *The Slave* is really Walker's monologue. Herein lies the major flaw of the play. In the manner of a defective "drama of ideas," the characters are too obviously mere ethical positions, not people. Grace, the ex-wife, and Easley, ex-teacher of Walker and now-husband of Grace, are very nearly reduced to personified abstractions. They too statically represent the *thought* of the detested liberals and apolitical esthetes. This is especially the case with Easley.

What the play loses in characterization, however, the dramatist tries to restore with such traditional devices as suspense and graphic stage effects, both of which surpass similar methods in Baraka's earlier plays. As Roland Reed points out, Baraka manages to provide some tension by having Walker become inebriated while he terrorizes the Easleys. In this manner, he not only gives Walker an excuse for openly talking about his and Grace's past, but he also equalizes the antagonists and prepares us for what we feel will be at least a plausible clash. The effeminate Easley should be almost a match for a drunken Walker, despite Walker's gun. By ending the first act with Walker in a stupor and Easley advancing on him, Baraka shows the same sense for dramatic timing that characterized the scenic organization of *Dutchman*. The frequent explosions, coming closer and closer to the house and represented by lighting effects as well as by sound, all give some life to an otherwise static play. These effects climax in the concluding scene in which the house is actually hit and Grace dies under a fallen beam.

We know almost from the start of the central action of the play that the basic conflict is essentially the same as that seen in the poems. The only difference lies in the dramatic representation of the frequently-accused "friends" of the poet. Grace and Easley are clearly their surrogates. Like the friends who feel that the poet has "thrown his life away" or that he is "no longer a credit to his race," Grace and Easley lament Walker's reorientation. Easley, whose name suggests the non-involved "luxury" so despised by the enraged Clay as well as the superficiality and comfortable status of the professor and poet, takes it for granted that Walker is dead as an artist because of his activist posture:

> You're not still writing . . . now are you? I should think the political, now military estates would be sufficient. And you always used to speak of the Renaissance as an evil time. And now you're certainly the gaudiest example of Renaissance man I've heard of.

Like the artist friends of the poet, Grace and Easley, moreover, scorn Walker's involvement with unsavory activist types. Easley defends Grace's desertion of Walker on the following grounds:

> [. . .] you pushed Grace until she couldn't retain her sanity and stay with you in that madness. All the bigoted racist imbeciles you started to cultivate. Every white friend you had knows that story.

Grace seconds this with:

> You began to align yourself with the worst kind of racists and second rate hack political thinkers.

The arguments of Grace and Easley are, of course, corollary to their esthetic principles, principles that Walker once shared. These principles will no longer suffice for Walker. They, too, are luxuries which the revolutionary cannot afford. Concerned only with the practical, the useful, Walker, like his creator, wants "an art that will function" (see note 20). In his condemnation of Easley, we hear echoes of the poet's attack on the evasive "talkers" of "Green Lantern's Solo" and "Balboa, the Entertainer." Walker tells Easley:

> You never did anything concrete to avoid what's going on now. Your sick liberal lip service to whatever was the least filth. Your high aesthetic disapproval of the political. Letting the sick ghosts of the thirties strangle whatever chance we had.

It is Walker's impatience with "lip service" that prompts him to insist, maniacally, that Easley die in silence. After shooting Easley, Walker shouts "Shut up, you! You shut up. I don't want to hear anything else from you. You just die, quietly. No more talk."

Walker's incessant attacks on Easley's manhood are quite interesting in light of the earlier plays, *The Baptism* and *The Toilet*. In those works, we recall, homosexuality was metaphor for the ultimate manifestation of manhood, *i.e.*, the demonstration of a truly humanistic, uninhibited, loving response. In referring to Easley as Grace's "faggot husband," however, we see a complete reversal of this metaphor. Easley's implied homosexuality is symbol of his moral failure, his refusal to care.

Walker recalls other friends from his pre-revolutionary days. They are epitomized in the writer Louie Rino, who "said . . . that he hated people who wanted to change the world." Aware that Rino's pronouncement represented the collective thought of his artist friends, Walker says:

> [. . .] I thought then that none of you would write any poetry either. I knew that you had moved too far away from the actual meanings of life . . . into some lifeless cocoon of pretended intellectual and emotional achievement, to really be able to see the world again. What was Rino writing before he got killed? Tired eliptical little descriptions of what he could see out the window.

(Judging from the description of Rino's verse, it must have been quite similar to, perhaps, Baraka's "The Clearing," a poem from *Preface*.) Though Walker says that such poetry holds no attraction for him and that the esthete within him is dead, he, nevertheless, continues to show a weakness for the old way and the insensitive order that it represents. Walker's split psyche is laid bare in his strangely apologetic remarks to Easley. Because of some prophetic or messianic imperative, Walker says that he must carry out the work of the revolution:

> [. . .] despite the fact that all of my officers are ignorant mother-fuckers who have never read any book in their lives, despite the fact that I would rather argue politics or literature, or boxing, and anything, with you dear Easley, with you. . . .

Walker's problem is quite like that of the guilt-ridden protagonist of *The Toilet*. The play strongly suggest that Walker's most difficult task will lie in coming to terms with his black brethren. He is still bound to the system that he finds so repugnant. This is most obvious in his lingering attraction for the cerebration and reflection so abhorred in the poems of *The Dead Lecturer* and *Sabotage*. It is this attraction that threatens the carrying out of the necessary revolutionary action. In the words of Walker, "Right is in the act! And the act itself has some place in the world . . . it makes some place for itself." Easley (freedom from toil) and Grace (simultaneously suggesting the blessing of whiteness or form above matter) continue to threaten Walker's commitment to action and self-assertion. Because they so graphically personify the detested elements of his inner being, they must die.

The complexity of this symbolic bondage is given additional emphasis in the characterization of Grace. It is obvious that Walker still loves Grace. He has even tried to continue their relationship along with his political activities. At one point he screams, "I never stopped telling you I loved you . . . or that you were my wife!" Grace's response that this "wasn't enough" is a poignant expression of the author's grim outlook upon the American racial situation. Even love (despite the protestations of Baldwin, King, and others) cannot free us from our tragic racial legacy. Grace rejects Walker's love and sides with the "three hundred years of oppression" that he attempts to eradicate. In this respect, she is not unlike Lula. Walker also shows his kinship to Clay in his inability to kill Grace, as well as in the concern he shows at the moment of her death.

With Grace's death, we are faced with the puzzling (and dramatically unsatisfying) implication that the children have met death at the hands of their father. In spite of Walker's earlier claim that he wants to take the girls with him, we are left with the impression that he has killed them. This would seem to be an impossible act for Walker, who cannot bring himself to kill the mother of his children and who kills the detested Easley only in drunken fear for his own life. This final scene is given an even greater ambiguity, however, in the concluding stage directions, ". . . *there is a child heard crying and screaming as loud as it can.*" Although there is nothing that says this child is one of the daughters, there is nothing, on the other hand, that says it is not. This seems to be a pointless ambiguity and not at all like the conclusion to *Dutchman*, which, although open to varying interpretations, allows for some kind of resolution in the mind of the viewer. Nevertheless, whether the girls are alive or dead, Walker leaves the Easley apartment, presumably freed of his past.

No longer the assimilationist but not yet completly belonging to those "ignorant motherfuckers who have never read a book in their lives," Walker is indeed representative of his creator at this stage of his career. He is not the unmitigated black hero of some interpretations. Consider John Lindberg's deification of Walker. He says: ". . . . while Clay falls easily to Lula's knife because he admires her whiteness, Walker kills his children to free himself from all white taint. He has become the man without a past, the stone revolutionist, Clay no more. This totally new man, committed to a historical imperative has passed beyond conventional human roles."[24] Baraka, despite his revolutionary fervor at this point, distinctly suggests that this is as much cause for weeping as rejoicing. Walker has paid a tremendous price for his freedom. Because he *must* work for the success of a revolution that will, in his words, "only change . . . the complexion of tyranny," he ends up locked in a hatred tantamount to that which marred the old order. Walker is a slave to his mission of hate. Hence, he exits as "*the old man at the beginning of the play.*"

Baraka, himself, at this point in his career, is a man between two worlds. In a surrogate manner, Walker burns the old bridges for his creator, who is yet without a new one. In the ensuing works, we see evidence of the author's attempting to immerse himself totally in the Black struggle.

Notes

[1]Isabel Eberstadt, "King of the East Village," *New York Herald Tribune*, 13 December 1964, Sunday Magazine Section, p. 13.

[2]Harold Cruse, *The Crisis of the Negro Intellectual* (New York: William Morrow and Company, inc., 1967), O. 356.

[3]Cheryl Lynn Munro, "LeRoi Jones: A Man in Transition," *College Language Arts Journal*, XVII, no, 1 (September, 1973): 64

[4]Richard Howard, *Nation*, CC, ii (15 March 1965): 289.

[5]LeRoi Jones, "The Myth of a Negro Literature," *Home* (New York: William Morrow and Company, 1966), p. 38.

[6]Diane Middlebrook, "David Henderson's Holy Mission," *Saturday Review*, 9 September 1972, p. 38.

[7]Art Berger, "Negroes with Pens," *Mainstream*, Vol. 16, no. 7 (July, 1963): 3.

[8]LeRoi Jones, *Blues People* (New York: William Morrow and Company, 1963), p. 228.

[9]Fischer, *Massachusetts Review*, 290.

[10]LeRoi Jones, "Black Writing," *Home* (New York: Morrow, 1966), p. 164.

[11]LeRoi Jones, "LeRoi Jones Talking," *Home* (New York: Morrow, 1966) p. 183

[12]LeRoi Jones, "The Last Days of the American Empire," *Home* (New York: Morrow, 1966), p. 195-96.

[13]*Encyclopedia Britannica*, Volume XI (Chicago, 1973), p. 434.

[14]Donald Costello, "Black Man as Victim," in Five Black Writers, ed: Donald Gibson (New York: New York University Press, 1970), p. 207.

[15]Hugh Nelson, "LeRoi Jones's *Dutchman*: a Brief Ride on a Doomed Ship," *Educational Theatre Journal*, XX (March, 1968): 54.

[16]E. Franklin Frazier, *Black Bourgeoisie* (New York: Collier Press, 1968), pp. 185-86.

[17]LeRoi Jones, "The Myth of a Negro Literature," *Home* (New York: Morrow, 1966), pp. 107-8.

[18]LeRoi Jones, "LeRoi Jones Talking," *Home* (New York: Morrow, 1966), pp. 187-88.

[19]C. W. E. Bigsby, *Confrontation and Commitment* (Columbia: University of Missouri Press, 1967), p. 155.

[20]LeRoi Jones, "The Revolutionary Theatre," *Home* (New York: Morrow, 1966), 210, 211, 212, 215.

[21]Ronald Gray, *Bertolt Brecht* (Edinburgh, Scotland: Grove Press, 1961), p. 62.

[22]*Ibid.*, 62.

[23]*Ibid.*, 62.

[24]John Lindberg, "*Dutchman* and *The Slave*, Companions in Revolution," *Black Academy Review*, Vol. 2, no. H1 (Spring-Summer, 1971): 106.

Chapter III

Imamu

[. . .] we labor
to make our getaway, into
The ancient image, into a new

correspondence with ourselves
and our black family. We need magic
now we need the spells, to raise up
return, destroy, and create. What will be

the sacred words?

The works to be considered in this chapter, *i.e.*, the poems and
plays that follow *The Slave*, are evidence of the author's arrival at a
thoroughly politicized art. Exemplary of Baraka's most didactic manner, the efforts are, generally speaking, directed to a black audience.
Although it is generally felt that the author sacrifices much of his
artistry in these simpler, "instructive" writings, it is my hope to
point out certain compensating strengths. To be sure, the intriguing
complexities (snytactic and symbolic) of the earlier poems are all too
frequently replaced by an overly simplistic didacticism. Similarly,
the plays often lack the abundant psychological implications of the
earlier works (*Great Goodness of Life* affords us ample proof that
this is not *always* the case). On the positive side, however, we see in
the ensuing poems a more inventive and faithful employment of the
crackling and essentially poetic language of the streets. Moreover,
these poems, and the plays as well, exemplify the author's considerable satiric powers. In this respect, they are reminiscent of the poet's
darkly humorous earliest works. Finally, I hope to show in this consideration of the latter agit-prop plays the artist's appropriation of
various theatrical conventions, a most ironical factor in light of the

strong "anti-Western" theme in these works.

Baraka's first programmatic application of his desire for "an art that will function" was seen in his work with The Black Arts Repertory Theatre/School, located in Harlem. Although this enterprise was not formally announced until February of 1965, Larry Neal, a close associate of the artist, states in "The Black Arts Movement" that the BART/S opened in "the spring of 1964"[1] under the leadership of Baraka, Charles Patterson, William Patterson, Clarence Reed, Johnny Moore, and others. Regarding the initial leadership of BART/S, however, Hudson is closer to the fact when he says, "Ostensibly, Jones went to Harlem to conduct the Black Arts Repertory Theater/School (BART/S). It is not true that he went to Harlem for the express purpose of founding this Theater/School, for it had been in existence in late 1964, while he was still living in the Village."[2] At any rate, when Baraka left the Village to take up residence "Uptown," he carried with him a passionate desire to "raise the consciousness" of a divided and debased people. The BART/S was surely an attractive vehicle in light of the artist's insistence that:

> . . . the socio-political must be wedded to the cultural. The socio-political must be a righteous extension of the cultural, as it is, legitimately, with national groups . . . A culturally aware black politics would use all the symbols of the culture, all the keys and images out of the black past, out of the black present, to gather the people to it, and energize itself with their strivings at conscious blackness. E. G.: Black art—the recreation of our lives, as black . . . to inspire, educate, delight and move black people. It is easier to get people into a consciousness of black power, what it is, by emotional example than through dialectical lecture. Black people seeing the recreation of their lives are struck by what is wrong or missing in them.[3]

The BART/S, then, afforded the artist a laboratory in which to test the compatibility of the cultural and socio-political, especially as it related to the edification of a largely unlettered audience. According to Larry Neal, the BART/S, under Baraka's leadership, was a success. He says: ". . . the Black Arts Theater took its programs into the streets of Harlem. For three months, the theater presented plays, concerts, and poetry readings to the people of the community. Plays that shattered the illusions of the American body politic, and awakened Black People to the meaning of their lives."[4]

In financial straits, the BART/S resorted to aid from OEO for its 1965 summer program. These funds were cut off when word got out that Baraka and his colleagues were teaching Harlemites to hate whites, with financing from the United States government. Details of this episode may be found in Hudson's study and Loften Mitchell's *Black Drama*. The premature death of BART/S was caused by more than financial problems, however. There is strong indication that the leaders of the theater grew further and further apart ideologically. Hudson discusses Baraka's hasty retreat to his hometown of Newark in the following manner:

> there are those . . . who will say that Jones was physically attacked by "friends" in Harlem in connection with their efforts to control Jones and BART/S for financial or political reasons. One person believes that Jones fled to Newark because of danger to his person. Another source hints that the basic friction was over whether BART/S would be essentially a tool or front for revolutionists. All of this, though, is hearsay, and should be considered as such. It is included here only as an indication of the currents of opinions and rumors concerning the people connected with BART/S.[5]

Though short-lived, the BART/S was an extremely influential endeavor. Black theater groups were formed all across the country as a result of the Harlem experiment. Following Baraka's example were groups on the West Coast, in Detroit, Philadelphia, Jersey City, New Orleans, and Washington, D. C. Groups also sprang up on such college campuses as San Francisco State College, Fisk University, Lincoln University, Hunter College, Columbia University, and Oberlin College.

Not only did such groups inspire and delight black people, they also served the very vital function of preparing talented apprentices for work in the theater. This, too, was one of Baraka's original intentions, as evidenced in the formal announcement of the BART/S's opening: "Acting, writing, directing, set designing, production, management and workshops will be openly aimed at gathering young Negroes interested in entering the professional theater world . . . . It also will provide already proven black dramatic talent with a showcase, as well as a cultural center for all the performing arts."[6]

There is considerable evidence to show that these practical goals were widely achieved. This is especially true in the case of black theater in New Orleans, the area most familiar to this writer. New Orleans boasted two black theater groups, the Dashiki Project Theater and the Free Southern Theater, the second of which was born during the height of the Civil Rights Movement, suffered decline along with the movement, and was rejuvenated in the wake of the Baraka-influenced renaissance in black theater. The high quality of Dashiki productions is attested to in their co-billing alongside the established New Orleans Repertory Theater during the summer of 1970. Dashiki's most successful production was *El Hajj Malik*, Clive Barnes says of the New York performance of this play by Dashiki playwright, N. R. Davidson:

> Political theater at its most fascinating is now to be found at the Martinique Theater, where last night the Afro-American Studio from Harlem brought its intellectually and emotionally provocative production of *El Hajj Malik*. . . .
>
> The play has been written by N. R. Davidson, Jr., whom I have not heard of before, and about whom the playbill is white and silent where it should have been black and noisy. He has constructed a kind of documentary picture of Malcolm that is both vivid and effective. . . .
>
> However, *El Hajj Malik*. . . . is more than just a documentary. Mr. Davidson has used (documentary) material to fill out an essentially ritualized poetic mosaic of his hero.[7]

Like BART/S, on which it was modeled, the Dashiki Project endeavor afforded its young and unknown writers a theatrical laboratory, and with the successful New York production of *El Hajj Malik*, this influence came full circle. Many of the blacks now acting and writing for stage and film received their fundamental training in such black community theaters, of which BART/S was prototype.

On his return to Newark, Baraka continued his community-oriented theatrical work with the organization of Spirit House and his troup of actors called "The Spirit House Movers." The experience gained in the BART/S project was of extreme importance in the formation of Spirit House, which was described in the following manner:

Spirit House is a black theater owned by the people of the community.
It's the only one in Newark. We have a repertory system—we not only
change the plays but we have films or poetry readings or lectures as well.
Anything the community wants—sports, music, parties, meetings, classes;
something is going on every night. The plays are only on weekends. We
have a permanent ensemble of actors; they're in most of the plays, and
of course, we use a lot of kids. We do a lot of children's plays, too. We
don't use Actor's Equity members: we don't have anything to do with
that; that's another world.[8]

Baraka's desire to organize the black community of Newark
was quickened during his brief stay in San Francisco in 1967. While
teaching at San Francisco State College, the artist met cultural nationalist Ron Karenga and closely observed the workings of Karenga's "US" organization. Baraka returned to Newark and organized
the Black Community Development and Defense Organization in
1968, under the influence of the teachings of Karenga. The BCD
members were adherents of the Kawaida faith, in which Baraka
served as priest. According to Hudson, Kawaida is a "contrived" religion, a conclusion that seems to be borne out by Baraka's own
statements regarding its practical nature. In an interview, Baraka told
Hudson that Kawaida is "a form . . . useful in a total social sense";
moreover, it "takes into consideration a kind of moral discipline of
orthodox Islam and African concepts that are useful to us."[9] Elsewhere, Baraka loosely described Kawaida as "that which is customary, or traditionally adhered to by black people."[10] The practitioners of Kawaida evidenced their adherence by wearing African garb,
speaking Swahili, and taking Islamic names. Everett LeRoi Jones became Ameer Baraka, *i.e.,* "blessed prince." To announce his priestly
emergence, he later added the title Imamu, *i.e.,* "spiritual leader."
Ameer was later changed to Amiri, with no change in meaning.

While involving himself with the spiritual, Baraka did not ignore the demands of the here-and-now. The man who so vehemently
scorned the system in his earlier essays became an astute practical
politician. David Llorens described Baraka's Newark organization in
the following manner: "The BCD, along with some 28 organizations,
including the politically mobilized United Brothers, make up the
Committee for United Newark which, according to its proposal for
the city, has as its main thrusts providing Communications, Voter
Education, and Voter Registration. The goal is the securing of political power for the Black and Puerto Rican communities."[11] The suc-

cess of this effort was most graphically seen in the 1970 election of Kenneth Gibson, Newark's first black major. Baraka's political involvement was manifested also in his efforts toward both national and international black organization. He co-chaired the 1972 Black Political Convention in Gary, Indiana and, later, worked in behalf of the Congress of African People.

In spite of this intense political involvement, Baraka continued to write poems and plays, works just as representative of the writer's changing psychic stance as were the earlier works. *Target Study* and *Black Art* (both collected in *Black Magic Poetry 1961-67*), *It's Nation Time*, and *In Our Terribleness* all show that Baraka's poetry, in particular, reflects the artist's movement from Beat poet to revolutionary poet-priest. The earliest post-Village works resemble the previously considered works of self-accusation. If anything, these poems are even more persistent in their dissection of the self and old motives. At the same time, the speaker of these poems accentuates the satisfying effect of his new vantage point and makes frequent lyrical forays into his personal past as well as that of collective black America. Along with these more lyrical moments, we see also an increase in the raw exhortations of the committed revolutionary. Much of the latter work is characterized by an increased employment of the street idiom and traditional black oral modes. There is also a markedly "spiritual" thrust in much of the "revolutionary" verse. The influence of orthodox Muslim doctrine, as well as the teachings of Elijah Muhammad, is apparent in this work. It is somewhat ironic that these efforts contain some of the artist's weakest poetry. Much of this verse, written by the assured spiritual leader, lacks the animating tension which marked the period of search. However, some of Baraka's best poetry since *The Dead Lecturer* appears in *In Our Terribleness*, wherein he synthesizes his more imaginative usage of the street idiom with the tendency toward spiritual exhortation.

In "Numbers, Letters," obviously an early post-Village work and the first poem of *Target Study*, Baraka reveals the pervasiveness of his debt to Whitman. Foremost in this poem is the writer's concern with the relationship of the "simple, separate person" to the all. Moreover, the poem evinces the progression of the characteristic Whitman poem, *i.e.*, the movement from a constricting but necessary self-discovery and acknowledgement to a more expansive and transcendent rebirth. Baraka begins by subjecting his "prodigal" soul to an exacting inquisition. To be sure, the questions are directed to the various discarded masks, the "schwartze bohemien" of "Hymn for Lanie Poo," Walker Vessels of *The Slave*, and Ray of *The Toilet*:

> If you're not home, where
> are you? Where'd you go? What
> were you doing when gone? When
> you come back better make it good.
> What was you doing down there, freakin' off
> with white women, hangin' out
> with Queens, say it straight to be
> understood straight, put it flat and real
> in the street where the sun comes and the
> moon comes and the cold wind in winter
> waters your eyes. Say what you mean, dig
> it out put it down, and be strong
> about it.

These and most of the following lines are marked by a syntactic simplicity only occasionally found in the earlier verse. This aspect is emphasized in the poet's insistence that he "say it straight to be/understood straight." There is also evidence of the poet's more concerted attempt to capture the street idiom. This is the function not only of the word omission of the fourth line, the grammatically incorrect question of the fifth line, the dropping of the "g's" in the slang usages "freakin' off" and "hangin' out," and the use of the slang term "Queens" to refer to former homosexual associates. It is also apparent in the cumulative effect of the statement, especially lines seven through thirteen. There is the black American's delight in the word music produced by such traditionally poetic devices as repetition ("say it straight to be/understood straight") and consonance ("straight," "street"). Linguistic variety is accentuated also in the last five lines, wherein a poignant lyricism gives way abruptly to a markedly staccato charge. The effect is not unlike that achieved by the more imaginative of black preachers.

The poet continues his dialogue with the self in lines that recall the furious passage studied in the preceding chapter:

> I cant say who I am
> unless you agree I'm real

> I cant be anything I'm not

He continues with striking lines of self-acknowledgement:

> I'm Everett LeRoi Jones, 30 yrs old.
> A black nigger in the universe. A long breath singer,
> wouldbe dancer, strong from years of fantasy
> and study.

These lines also reflect the culmination of the writer's long struggle with the question of his identity. Moreover, they indicate Baraka's belief that the black writer must proudly accept himself if he is ever to produce a significant literature. Compare the last quoted lines to the following excerpt from Baraka's "Philistinism and the Negro Writer":

> The Negro middle class realized that in a society where black is a liability, the coolest thing is not to be that, so the first thing the Negro writer has to say is, "Well, I am a Negro," which is a great, dramatic thing. To say that is to realize that it means not only some racial delineation, but a responsibility to a specific and particular culture, one that can be talked about meaningfully, simply because it is a human experience—your human experience.[12]

Hence, "I am Everett LeRoi Jones [. . .] /A black nigger in the universe."

The poet ends this lyrical manifesto with a return to the familiar conflict between the demands of thought and feeling, so often visible in the works of *Sabotage* and *The Dead Lecturer*. He informs us that he is no longer ruled by the tyranny of cogitation. The feelings are no longer subjugated to the intellect. After achieving this Whitmanesque equipoise, the poet goes on to manifest a degree of openness or transcendence of self not present in the earlier lines. This rebirth is even reflected in the ecstatically expansive conclusion:

> I am a meditative man. And when I say something it's all of me saying, and all the things that make me, have formed me, colored me this brilliant reddish night. I will say nothing I feel is lie. . . . .
> My heart is large as my mind
> this is a messenger calling, over here, over here, open your eyes and your ears and your souls; today is the history we must learn to desire. There is no guilt in love.

This insistence on the need to incorporate thought with feeling is expressed also in the frequently anthologized "young Soul," which immediately follows "Numbers, Letters" in *Target Study*. This exhortation to black youth ends:

> Make some muscle
> in your head, but
> use the muscle
> in yr heart

Like "Numbers, Letters," "Tele/vision," another backward glance, is also a rather paradoxical poem of recantation and acceptance. As cognizant of figures from popular culture as ever, the poet looks back in pain to the time when he was:

> . . . sammy davis
> for allen ginsbergs frank sinatra. the beginning
> of the alien.

In lines recalling *The Toilet*, the poet examines his adolescent years. The programmed son of the black middle class is described as:

> . . . winded-up-leroy heading down belmont avenue
> thinking he was grey. James Edward's nose was too ugly hunched
>   open
> like that. And the other dude, the doctor, calling him dirty names
> invisible kike of the mind.
>   . . . . I limped along with
> the rest of the niggers, and was beautiful then to invisible greys.
> They found me, found each at the end of the long slaughter house.
> Who will save the jesusnigger? Who will come back smiling and lick-
>   ing
>   him silent knowledge?
> Who will be the final coming attraction and beautiful character actor
> of my bonafide creation? The me's of it. The strong I's. Yell. They
>   CRAAAAAAAYYYY
> YYYYYYYYYVE to good faith blessing. Ahhh. The nature. The
> smell. I
>   am whole
> I am whole.

Again we remark the pervasiveness of popular culture imagery. As in the earliest poems, the poet gauges his own awareness of self and the world by his response to figures from movies and comics. Here the poet is obviously recalling the movie "Home of the Brave," in which black actor James Edwards starred. The "winded-up-leroy," filled with cultural shame, found the too-negroid features of Edwards repulsive. The "doctor" of these lines is obviously the psychiatrist who attempts to heal Edwards of his paralysis by provoking him with racial insults.

Baraka shows here his increasingly anti-semitic posture by referring to the psychiatrist as the "invisible kike of the mind." Although the poet declares his abhorrence of various "niggers," "wops," and "greys" in general, his anti-semitism seems to surpass his intolerance for the other groups and assumes its rankest form in "For Tom Postell, Dead Black Poet." This is, of course, an extension of the earlier rejection of his artistic peers, who were, generally speaking, Jewish "liberals."

> Now they ask me to be a jew or italian, and turn from the moment disappearing into the shaking clock of treasonable safety, ...

In the increasingly anti-intellectual poems that follow, the Jew is censured as the epitome of reflection, and, thus, of decadence. There is also the factor of the dissolution of the poet's marriage to his Jewish wife, the particulars of which we can never and, perhaps, need never know. Nevertheless, the roots of the poet's attitude regarding Jews undoubtedly stems, at least in part, from the negative effects of earlier relationships.

The "doctor" of the quoted passage, as well as the "greys" referred to later, is "invisible" to the young poet because the poet was not able to perceive their treachery, *i.e.*, the death they intended for him. Like Ray of *The Toilet*, the poet was the "jesusnigger," the black held in adoration for his assimilable nature. He informs us, however, that he has escaped the transforming (in "good faith") zeal of the missionaries, and he celebrates this escape in an ecstatic manner recalling the concluding lines of "Numbers, Letters."

The poems of recantation are often sharply focused on the old haunts and the poet's "lost" friends, the *avant-garde* artists. In "A

School of Prayer," one of the writer's more blatantly prosaic pieces,
he says:

> Do not obey their laws
> which are against God.
> [. . .]
> Their "laws" are filthy evil,
> against almighty God. They are
> sick to be against God,
> [. . .]
> against thought and feeling
> against the world as it most commonly
> is. That is they are against
> beauty. Do not let them show you
> a beer can, except believe their profundity
> is as easily read. Do not believe or shelter them.

The injunction against the anti-humanism of *avant garde* artistry, so
prevalent in *The Dead Lecturer*, is continued here in the attack on
the painter or sculptor who, is the manner of Andy Warhol, produces
an absolute duplication of Ballantine's or Campbell's packaged products. In Baraka's vision, this is not only the ultimate manifestation
of artistic insipidity but also symbolic proof that art in America is
simply another servant of commerce. This thesis reminds us of "The
Politics of Rich Painters," a poem from *The Dead Lecturer*.

The poet expresses his contempt for the esthetes in yet
another glance back at the ruinous influence of the old milieu, and
although the poet does not designate her so, we know that he again
speaks of Crow Jane:

> the great witch of euro-american legend
> who sucked the life
> from some unknown nigger
> whose name will be known
> but whose substance will not ever
> not even by him
> who is dead in a pile of dopeskin

The utter destruction of this particular casualty is underscored in the
gnawingly repetitive cadence of these lines, especially the third
through the sixth. Giving the particulars, the poet explains further:

This bitch killed a friend of mine named Bob Thompson
a black painter, a giant, once, she reduced
to a pitiful imitation faggot
full of American holes and a monkey on his back
slapped airplanes
from the empire state building

Like Billie Holiday and Charlie Parker, Bob Thompson, black artist in a hostile environment, fell prey to drugs. The poet expresses this tragedy with his old wry humor, which is again dependent both on the imagery of popular culture and the street idiom. Thompson had more than the average junky's habit, *i.e.*, "monkey on his back." To adequately describe the enormity of the painter's addiction, the poet invokes the image of King Kong. As in the Crow Jane poems, he projects a death for the bitch goddess, a death that will be occcasioned this time, however, by his imprecations:

May this bitch and her sisters, all of them,
receive my words
in all their orifices like lye mixed with
cocola and alaga syrup

feel this shit, bitches, feel it, now laugh your
hysterectic laughs
while your flesh burns
and your eyes peel to red mud.

Here we see the poet resorting to the blackest of humor, *i.e.*, in terms of race as well as the morbidly comic. First, the poet's ear for the nuances of black speech is strikingly apparent in the lone word "cocola." The second syllable of this venerable trade name is rarely heard in the pronunciation of blacks, particularly southern blacks. Black associations are brought out also in the mention of another familiar trade name, Alaga (for Alabama-Georgia) syrup, *the* syrup used by serious eater of pancakes. We see also in the punning "hysterectic" a likely black "misuse" of the language.

In the poem "Western Front," Baraka assails his old artistic orientation by personally attacking the poet he once described as the "only . . . . white man in New York I really trust—that's Allen Ginsberg. I trust him and love him completely. . . ." We recall that the early poem "One Night Stand," a tempered, brotherly rebuff, was dedicated to Ginsberg. In "Western Front," however, Baraka bitterly indicts his former associate for his mid-sixties emergence as the irresponsible, euphoric guru of the drug cult:

> Poems are made
> by fools like Allen Ginsberg, who loves God, and went to India
> only to see God, finding him walking barefoot in the street,
> blood sickness and hysteria, yet only God touched this poet,
> who has no use for the world. But only God, who is sole dope
> manufacturer of the universe, and is responsible for ease and
> logic. Only God, the baldhead faggot, is clearly responsible,
> not, for definite, no cats we know.

In place of the artistry so vehemently rejected in the previous poems, Baraka begins to posit more forcefully a socially and politically committed poetry. His new poetic manifesto, reminiscent of his call for a "revolutionary theater," is expressed in the poem "Black Art." Baraka says:

> Poems are bullshit unless they are
> teeth or trees or lemons piled
> on a step. Or black ladies dying
> of men leaving nickel hearts beating
> them down.

The poem itself must be just as concrete, just as real, as those interminable artifacts spoken of in "How You Sound" (see note 24, Chapter I). Moreover, poems must be put to human use:

> Fuck poems
> and they are useful, wd they shoot
> come at you, love what are are,
> breathe like wrestlers, or shudder
> strangely after pissing.

The bold metaphors of bodily functions force upon us an understanding of the poet's uncompromisingly humanistic demands for the poem. Baraka demands also that the revolutionary poem spare no one in its apocalyptic thrust. The black, the Jew, the Italian, and the Irishman—each in his turn—are all reduced to the lowest sterotypes:

> We want poems
> like fists beating niggers out of Jocks
> or dagger poems in the slimy bellies
> of the owner-jews. Black poems to
> smear on girdlemamma mullatto bitches
> whose brains are red jelly stuck
> between 'lizabeth taylor's toes. Stinking
> Whores! We want "poems that kill."
> Assassin poems, Poems that shoot
> guns. Poems that wrestle cops into alleys
> and take their weapons leaving them dead
> with tongues pulled out and sent to Ireland. Knockoff
> poems for dope selling wops or slick halfwhite
> politicians Airplane poems, rrrrrrrrrrrrrrrr
> rrrrrrrrrrrrrrr . . . tuhtuhtuhtuhtuhtuhtuhtuhtuh
> . . . rrrrrrrrrrrrrrrr . . . Setting fire and death to
> whities ass.

The "niggers" in Jocks are, on the one hand, middle class blacks who squander valuable time attempting to be seen in those places frequented by the "smart set." From all indications, Jock's is just such a place (see "Unfinished," *Tales*). On the other hand, we see the playful hand of Baraka at work here. Niggers in "Jocks" could also be black athletes, the old heroes who were attacked with increasing frequency in nationalist quarters. The self-hatred of the "mulatto bitches," the distaff side of the Niggers in Jocks, is also treated in the humorous poem "W.W."

It goes without saying that every Jew is not a capitalistic exploiter, that every Italian is not a member of the mafia, that every Irishman is not an oppressive policeman, and that every black politician is not insensitive to the needs of his black constituents. The poet is simply attempting, through this overwrought and particularizing indictment, to show that no element in American society can hide from the righteous wrath of the enraged black writer. As suggested by the onomatopoeic sortie of the last quoted lines, this poem, as well as the poems to come, is an incendiary barrage aimed at all hostile influences on the black American's spiritual growth. In this poem, the author employs the oracular manner of the fire-and-brimstone preacher. Like the fundamentalist preacher, he builds his invocation through a passionate reliance on repetition and a perfect sense of timing. The crucial matter at hand, *i.e.*, poetry, is thrust upon the hearer's consciousness through repeated imploration. The word *Poem* very nearly appears in every statement of the poem itself. Baraka's poem (or mini-sermon) shows to great advantage the folk preacher's sense of timing. The emotional buildup (climaxing in the onomatopoeic barrage) and release (concluding in the calm coda) are indeed reminiscent of the most exemplary folk sermons.

Like "Black Art," "A Poem for Black Hearts," written in memory of Malcolm X, is a striking illustration of the poem put to political use. In the tradition of Wordsworth's paean to Toussaint L'Ouverture, this poem receives much of its force from the poet's employment of imagery suggesting the martyred leader's manly and unswerving dedication to the complete liberation of the black man:

> [. . .] For
> Malcolm's hands raised to bless us
> all black and strong in his image
> of ourselves, For Malcolm's words
> fire darts, the victor's tireless
> thrusts, words hung above the world
> change as it may, he said it, and
> for this he was killed, for saying,
> and feeling, and being/change, all
> collected hot in his heart [. . .]

Malcolm's *manhood*—no word is more charged with meaning in the latter works of Baraka—is held up as a challenge to black men. It is the standard to which the "victims" must aspire. The poem ends with a clarion call of mounting intensity, with staccato challenges gradually giving way to smoother entreatments. The poet implores the black man to discard the old images, the old masks:

> For all of him, and all of yourself, look up,
> black man, quit stuttering and shuffling, look up,
> black man, quit whining and stooping, for all of him,
> For Great Malcolm a prince of the earth, let nothing in us
> rest until we avenge ourselves for his death, stupid animals
> that killed him, let us never breathe a pure breath if we
> fail, and white men call us faggots till the end of the earth.

We see in works such as "Black Art" and "A Poem for Black Hearts" that the poet started to address himself specifically to the black audience around 1965-66. Much of the poetry of this period is characterized by the hortatory tone of the preceding lines, and much of it was obviously written for oral presentation. However, the poems of this period of the author's career do not always evince the artistry of the foregoing works. These works often manifest the overly prosaic style of "A School of Prayer." In spite of this they are often rather humorous. For example, "Black Bourgeoisie," a blistering attack on the despised "half-screamer," reads like the concluding lines of "Hymn for Lanie Poo." The pretender

> has a gold tooth, sits long hours
> on a stool thinking about money.
> sees white skin in a secret room
> rummages his sense for sense
> dreams about Lincoln(s)
> conks his daughter's hair
> sends his coon to school
> works very hard
> grins politely in restaurants
> has a good word to say
> never says it
> does not hate ofays
> hates, intead him self
> him black self

The artist assures the desired oral effect of this poem through his skillful employment of vowel patterns. The repeated long "o" sounds of the early lines reinforce the image of a somnambulistic, even drugged, individual. These sound patterns frequently do as much to create effect as do the words themselves. It is in poems like this one that we see most clearly Baraka's influence on the younger black poets, *i.e.*, Don Lee, Nikki Giovanni, Sonya Sanchez, and others. These poets took the humorously recriminatory "rap" to its limits. Like Baraka, these writers became as popular as some recording artists or sports figures in black communities across the country. Their works, too, were written for oral presentation and had a profound effect on a broad range of black auditors. For example, this writer witnessed Baraka's dramatic reading of "Poem for HalfWhite College students," a *performance* which delighted his audience of several hundred black college students. No visual reading could capture the theatrics of the poet as he, again with all the fervor of a black fundamentalist preacher, asks the students:

> How do you sound, your words, are they
> yours? The ghost you see in the mirror, is it really
> you, can you swear you are not an imitation greyboy,
> can you look right next to you in the chair, and swear,
> that the sister you have your hand on is not really
> so full of Elizabeth Taylor, Richard Burton is coming
> out of her ears.

Baraka's dogmatic versification on the "correct" black behavior is sometimes unbelievably narrow and short-sighted, as shown in the graffiti-like "Civil Rights Poem," reprinted here in its entirety:

> Roywilkins is an eternal faggot
> His spirit is a faggot
> his projection
> and image, this is
> to say, that if i ever see roywilkins
> imonna
> stick half my sandal
> up his
> ass

This kind of blatant put-down comprises much of the later pamphlet collections such as *It's Nation Time* (1970). In this work of the committed black nationalist, the nation-building plea goes out to all "lost" brothers. Note the humorous word-play in these lines, particularly the fragmented directive of the third and fourth lines:

> doctor nigger, please do somethin on we
> lawyer nigger, please pass some laws about us
> liberated nigger with the stringy haired mind, please lib lib lib
> you spliv er ate
> US, we you, [. . .]
> please mister liberated nigger love chil nigger
> nigger in a bellbotton bell some psychodelic wayoutness
> on YO People, even while you freeing THE People, [. . .]
> ple please [. . .]
>   newest negro to understand that theres no black
>   no white
> only people [. . .]

On occasion these attacks on "wrongheaded" blacks transcend
flippancy and show the full range of Baraka's power as a poet. The
poignant "Cops" is just such a poem. In this poem we see evidence of
Baraka's increasing employment of the narrative mode. Like the ball-
adeer of old, he realizes the powerful appeal of the narrative on the
imaginations of the illiterate or semi-literate audience. Although he
never communicates fully with this group, at least not in his poetry,
his increasing use of the narrative and dramatic modes must be seen
in terms of his attempt to do so. Much of the strength of "Cops"
stems from the poet's dramatic recollection of childhood memories
and his adept employment of the speech of the black urban hipster.
The latter is seen in the very first word of the poem, *i.e.*, "flyol-
floyd." In actuality this is three words—fly old Floyd—connected for
effect. The term "fly" is street argot for "ultra-hip." Baraka manages
to make Floyd even more street-wise by his swift combination.
Moverover, in a dramatic reading, the words would come out with
the rapidity suggested by the spelling. Floyd, former musician, lover,
and friend, was once "smooth as anything blowin. . . ." Now a brutal
policeman, *i.e.*, in Baraka's mind, a member of the repressive forces
in the black community, Floyd

> [. . .] weights 400 now
> and threatens junkies
> on Howard Street, calling them by first or nick
> names, really scaring the piss out of them, being
> "a Nice guy" and all his killings being accidental

Other former friends, now cops, are recalled. "Bowleg Otis"—
the poet's refusal to spell the name "Bowleg*ged*" is evidence of his
understanding of the speech of his subjects—is remembered as a
"prick" who arrested a "dude" he knew all his life. Leon is remembered for being a "bad," *i.e.*, "good" in the black idiom, catcher.
Moreover, he is said to have been "strong as a bitch," very nearly the
ultimate metaphorical compliment, surpassed only by the nonpareil
"motherfucker." Instead of describing yet another former friend as a
strange fellow, the poet recalls him as a "funnytime cat." Rather
than say that the boys often had sexual relations with this friend's
sister, he says, "Cats used to/pop his sister." In recalling the music
of his youth, his athletic involvement, and his early sexual experiences, the poet waxes nostalgic. All these memories are shattered, however, with the harsh realization of the completely alien nature of his

former peers. Fighting off the powerful desire to salvage at least a part of the past, to reestablish communication, the poet ends by asking himself:

> You wanna stand in front of a bar, with a gun
> pointed at you? You wanna try to remember why you liked some-
> body
> while the bullet comes. Shit.

Although the "committed" and hortatory poems are of uneven quality, Baraka continues to show his true poetic worth in those works concerned with the racial heritage, poems recalling "Poem for Willie Best" and "Three Modes of History and Culture." "Biography," "The Mighty Flight," and "Dada Zodji" evidence this concern. "Dada Zodji, the earliest of these, has as its theme the rape of Africa. The lines ring with the rich suggestiveness of Baraka's best creations. This is poetry for the eye as well as the ear:

> Ships crowd west, in long lines
> floating culture in. New ports and
> stalls, designed by disease and money

The suffering of the infamous "middle passage" is intimated in the following lines, lines recalling Robert Hayden's famed poem on this subject:

> [. . .] Ship lanes
> in straight lines. For harmony and
> the stacked deck of power's measure.
> "Millions killed themselves,"
>   in the dark. Jumping
> off buildings and boats

As in "Poem for Willie Best," the poet laments the loss of identity that came with the black man's enslavement. Stripped of the vital elements of his culture, he is left

> [. . .] with no tongue
> to give my children their names.

In spite of the appalling deprivations, the slave survived, a fact that never ceases to amaze and strengthen the poet, who accepts this survival as proof of the black man's central role in mankind's future salvation. He endured by:

> Claiming the useless parts of vegetables, and a music
> too close to hysteria.

"Biography" also voices the pervasive desolation of the black past. The symbolist suggestiveness of this poem leads us to the realization that Baudelaire left his mark on Clay and Clay's creator as well. The provocatively vague lines passionately convey the impression of a lynching. The anguish of the victim, the sinister atmosphere, and the festivity of the spectators are all keenly impled. Indeed, the very configuration of the words on the page reinforces the theme. The words dangle in a long, lean, suggestively dripping line.

> Hangs
> whipped blood striped
> meat pulled
> clothes ripped
> slobber
> feet dangled
> pointing
> noised
> noise
> churns
> face
> black sky
> and moon
> leather night
> red
> bleeds
> drips
> ground
> sucks
> blood
> hangs
> life wetting
> sticky
> mud
>
> laughs

        bonnets
        wolfmoon
        crazyteeth

        hangs

        hangs

        granddaddy
        granddaddy, they tore

        his
        neck

The grotesquerie and pathos of this poem are both underscored through the employment of incremental repetition ("hangs," "blood," "bleeds") and rhyme ("whipped," "ripped," "blood," "mud"). Both elements lend a globular weightiness to the truncated "lines," making each repeated usage of rhyme fall in a copiously suggestive manner. Moreover, the more freely spaced and syntactically conventional final lines suggest a gradual dissipation of the flow.

The poet expresses the strong conviction that no black man can ever afford to forget the atrocities. In "The Alternative" (*Tales*), the narrator censures the black college for attempting to blot out the harsher realities of the black past. The indictment bears a striking similarity to the poem just quoted. Baraka, one of the severest critics of the black college, feels that all too frequently black colleges have been monuments to "Silence, and a reluctance of Memory."[13] They would have their students "Forget the slow grasses, and flame, flame in the valley. Feet bound, dumb eyes begging for darkness. The bodies move with the secret movement of the air. Swinging Flame, flame in the valley."[14]

Baraka's sensitivity to the past is lyrically rendered in the pensive "leroy," occasioned by the poet's wistful study of the picture of his mother as a coed. He says:

    I wanted to know my mother when she sat
    looking sad across the campus in the late 20's
    into the future of the soul, there were black angels
    straining above her head, carrying life from our ancestors,

and knowledge, and the strong nigger feeling. She sat
(in the photo in the yearbook I showed Vashti) getting into
new blues, from the old ones, the trips and passions
showered on her by her own. Hypnotizing me, from so far
ago, from that vantage of knowledge passed on to her passed on
to me and all other black people of our time.

These lines exude a strong sense of continuity, which the poet art-
fully underscores in the parenthetical phrase of line six. Vashti, obviously a younger relative, will be the next to inherit the racial legacy, *i.e.*, the "strong nigger feeling," passed on to her from the ancestors, the poet's mother, and the poet himself. The poet concludes
with a powerful metaphorical rendering of his personal bequest:

When I die, the consciousness I carry I will to
black people. May they pick me apart and take the
useful parts, the sweet meat of my feelings. And leave
the bitter bullship rotten white parts
bullshit
alone.

The writer's feeling concerning the racial legacy carries over
into his attitude on his particular literary patrimony. In "That Mighty Flight," we see evidence of Baraka's shifting perspective concerning literature written by black Americans. The literature has taken on
more value and the artist sees himself as part of a significant artistic continuum. The poet expresses this new attitude in terms of his
relationship to Richard Wright and James Baldwin.

My brother, Bigger Thomas, son of
Poor Richard, father, of poor
lost jimmy, locked together all
of us, wringing our hands in the dark.
Lost to our selves and our poeple, that we find,
just few moments of life and light let it come
down, lord, that we love life more than all life
and want it, want our selves, and our black soul nation
to love us as great strong prophets and heroes, but weak
lord, we weak as flesh, fall sometimes, Bigger laughed
when the old jew left him, "a wry bitter smile," dug
we were flying, and his father, and brother, and the son's
son, all rising, lord to become the thing you told us

As in this poem, the allusions in the works of this stage of Baraka's career are drawn largely from the works of black authors. The shift from a white to black frame of reference is clearly presented in the stories and sketches of *Tales*, written over a number of years.

Baraka seeks to bind himself to black people, to show the finality of his return, not only by digesting and intoning the depth of his racial heritage but also by versifying some of the more characteristic examples of the vibrant black oral tradition. As Roger D. Abrahams assesses the importance of the black street idiom: "One of the dominant features of life style in most Afro-American communities is the continuing reliance on oral expression. This means that there is still a good deal of social value placed on verbal abilities; these can often be best exhibited in a contest fashion, contests which are waged in Creole or street language rather than standard English."15 Baraka shows in his "formalized" renderings of the "dozens" (see page *35*, Chapter I), "signifying," and "macking," that he, too, in spite of a tongue-in-cheek manner, places great value on certain oral modes and on the imaginative expressive powers of those schooled in the streets. This estimation is reflected in "Prettyditty," an example of the poet's ability with the dramatic poem. "Prettyditty" reads:

> Who were the guys
> who wrote, who winced around
> and thought
> about
> things? Oh, the kind of cats, you know wobbling
> through a crowd full of electric
> identifications, and the blessings
> of the planets? who said that, howd
> you get in this bar, what are you a
> smart dude, with his hair some kind
> a funny way, with his hand to prop
> ersition the enemies of grace amen
> music drowns us sit down anyway you
> louse, and you got a story, i got
> one he got one, and that bitch way cross
> there,
> she gott
> a mother
> fucker.

Here the poet deliberately deflates the concept of the "writer." The "guys/who wrote, who winced around/and thought/about things" are, like the ex-Village poet LeRoi Jones and his former associates, drunk with a false sense of personal importance. These lines appear to be spoken by at least two voices. Like "Cops," this poem seems to have been written with the semi-literate or illiterate auditor in mind. This work, too, has a concise "story" line, but rendered dramatically rather than narratively. The dramatic effect is underscored by strong implications of scene and atmosphere. Perhaps the poem is, like "Numbers, Letters," a dialogue with the self. At any rate, the voice that asks the first two questions is markedly different from the one that speaks from line eight to the poem's conclusion. Whether or not he accepts the "sacred" image of the writer, the first speaker sets off an intense reaction with his wistful question. In the parlance of the street, the second speaker "pulls [the first speaker's] coat," *i.e.*, enlightens him. Seemingly overhearing the first speaker's warped exhaltation of the "writer," he apprizes him of the viability of the unwritten or "street" tradition, wherein every man is a creator, a teller of tales. There is, moreover, the strong implication that these tellers have more potent tales because they are rooted in the reality of the teller's lives. It is very nearly impossible to explain the effect of the last three lines of the poem. However, anyone who has ever heard the black street idiom spoken will attest to the poet's unfailing ear in this particular instance. "She gott/a mother/fucker" roughly translates (and I emphasize "roughly"), "She has one hell of a story to tell." Stephen Henderson is correct when he says, " 'Prettyditty' hinges on the last line and especially on the hyperbolic but subtle ingroup meanings of 'motherfucker.' "[16]

In "T. T. Jackson Sings," we see Baraka's whimsical attempt to record a typical example of "dozens" rhyme, a special "genre" in the black oral tradition, already mentioned briefly in my discussion of *The Toilet*. Although there have been several scholarly treatments of the "dozens" and their psycho-social meaning, no one gives a better concise explanation of the game than does H. Rap Brown. He says in *Die Nigger Die*, his autobiography:

> The street is where young bloods get their education. I learned how to talk in the street, not from reading about Dick and Jane going to the zoo and all that simple shit. The teacher would test our vocabulary

each week, but we knew the vocabulary we need. They'd give us arithmetic to exercise our minds. Hell, we exercised our minds by playing
the dozens . . . . In many ways . . . the dozens is a mean game because
what you try to do is totally destroy somebody else with words . . .
It was a bad scene for the dude that was getting humuliated.[17]

Baraka's "T. T. Jackson Sings" evokes this very special
"schooling" spoken of by Brown. The poet shows the depth of his
acquaintance with his materials even in the title of the jingle. The
initials, T. T., stand for nothing other than T. T. Numerous black
men and boys bear the "names" T. T., O. C., J. D., C. L., *etc.* (these
being some of the more common combinations). In combining this
given "name" with the common black surname, Jackson, the poet
creates a powerfully composite black folk image. T. T.'s delivery is
standard.

> I fucked your mother
> on top of a house
> when I got through
> she thought she was
> Mickey Mouse
>
> I fucked your mother
> under a tree
> when it was over
> she couldn't even pee
> [. . .]

Baraka's poems occasionally take their shape from the venerable street practice of "signifying," which is a tactic employed in
verbal dueling. The "signifier" speaks in an indirect or coded manner
in order to change the behavior of his adversary. The "signifying"
comment is generally intended to shame or embarrass the adversary.
Sometimes the message is not very indirect or covert at all. Whether
speaking openly or slyly, the signifier's message is hortatory. He
wants to move his hearer to some desired course of action. It stands
to reason that Baraka, poet-turned-priest, should incorporate this
familiar mode in his didactic verse. "W. W." is a striking example of
the "signifying" poem.

> Back home the black women are all beautiful,

and the white ones fall back, cutoff from 1000
years stacked booty, and Charles of the Ritz
where Jooshladies turn into billy burke in blueglass
kicks. With wings, and jingly bew-teeful things.
The black women in Newark are fine. Even with all that grease
in their heads. I mean even the ones where the wigs
slide around, and they coming at you 75 degrees off course.
I could talk to them. Bring them around. To something.
Some kind of quick course, on the sidewalk, like Hey baby
why don't you take that thing off yo' haid. You look like
Miss Muffet in a runaway ugly machine. I mean. Like that.

Here we see the humor that was largely lacking in the poems discussed in the previous chapter. Note the wordplay, the alliterative ring of the first four lines, the use of slang, and the outrageously bizarre ending. In this poem, the speaker wants to awaken the black woman to an appreciation of her personal worth and natural beauty. The poet effectively invokes the pun in this effort. We see in the reference to the black woman's "1000/years stacked booty" a pointed *double entendre* indeed. "Booty" is a frequently used term for the posterior in black slang (recall the poet's earlier praise of "steatopygia" in "Hymn for Lanie Poo"). It is quite significant that the speaker of these lines would attempt to "Bring them around," *i.e.*, "pull their coats," on the sidewalk. Signifying is, after all, street talk. The poem ends with another characteristic element from the black oral tradition, the hyperbolic or nonsensical wisecrack. For verbal combatants, the stranger and more bizarre the comparison, the better. Such comparisons are frequently used in dozens rhymes. Like Baraka, Ralph Ellison shows an ear for this practice with his anonymous street character's description of Ras: "And man that crazy son of a bitch up there on that hoss looking like death eating a sandwich."[18]

A large number of the works of *Target Study* and *Black Art* reflect the angry mood of the black inner-city dweller of the mid and late '60's. Characteristic speakers in many of the poems are rioters or guerrila fighters. "Black People!" the consummate example of Baraka's "riot" poetry, is characterized by such a voice. Although this work perhaps lacks "poetic" metaphor, it is animated by the charged language and searing defiance that marked the firery "drama" acted out on the streets of American cities during the 1960's. The poem is perhaps best understood as counterstatement to

the well-known "rip-off" advertisements of the radio stations aimed
at the black communities across the country, advertisements infamous for duping the poor into purchases of shoddy goods and interminable payments. This work is actually a parody, an inverted "sales
pitch," spoken in the idiom of the black ghetto dweller. For example, the "bad short" of the first line is an attractive automobile:

> What about that bad short you saw last week
> on Frelinghuysen, or those stoves and refrigerators, record
> players in Sears, Bambergers, Klein's, Hahnes', Chase, and
> on Washington Street, and those couple shops on Springfield?
> You know how to get it, you can get it, no money never, money
> don't grow on trees no way, only whitey's got it, makes it
> with a machine, to control you, you cant steal nothin from a
> white man, he's already stole it he owes you anything you want,
> even his life. All the stores will open if you will say the
> magic words. The magic words are: Up against the wall mother
> fucker this is a stick up! . . .
> No money down. No time to pay. Just
> take what you want. The magic dance in the street. Run up and
> down Broad
> Street niggers, take the shit you want. . . .
> We must make our own
> World, man, our own world, and we cannot do this unless the white
> man
> is dead. Let's get together and killhim my man, let's get
> to gather the fruit
> of the sun, let's make a world we want black children to grow and
> learn in
> do not let your children when they grow look in your face and curse
> you by
> pitying your tomish ways.

Here the poet employs the strikingly theatrical method seen so often
in the works of this period. He visualizes a situation and literally
creates a mini-drama, complete with stage directions.

The same directive is seen in "Three Movements and a Coda,"
wherein the speaker describes his own riotous activity and exhorts
his listener in much the same manner as the last speaker:

> Came running out of the drugstore window with
> an electric alarm clock, and then dropped the motherfucker

and broke it. Go get somethin' else. Take everything in there.
Look in the cashregister. TAKE THE MONEY. TAKE THE
MONEY. YEH.
TAKE IT ALL. YOU DONT HAVE TO CLOSE THE DRAWER.
COME ON MAN, I SAW
A TAPE RECORDER BACK THERE.
> These are the words of lovers
> Of dancers, of dynamite singers
> These are songs if you have the
> music.

In this tranquil "coda," Baraka suggests that these acts of pillage are acts of self-creation, of righteous rage. However, there is also evidence in the poems of *Black Art* that the poet is rapidly coming to the conclusion that such materialistically oriented re-creation is not enough. He would administer to the spirits of men. Compare the lyrical "Distant Hearts, Come Close/r, in the Smash of Night" to the poems just cited. The exhortation is markedly different in this metaphorical and more conventionally "poetic" work:

> Our strength is in the drums,
> the sinuous horns, blow forever beautiful princes, touch
> the spellflash of everything, all life, and the swift go on
> go off and speed. Blow, forever, like the animals, plants and
> sun. Forever in our universe there is beauty and light, we come
> back to it now. Throwing off the tons of dumb metal the beast
> has strapped up in. Those Things. These refrigerators, stoves,
> automobiles, airships, let us return to the reality of spirit,
> to how our black ancestors predicted life should be, from the
> mind and the heart, our souls like gigantic kites sweep across
> the heavens, let us follow them, with our trembling love for
> the world. Let us look up at each other's spirits zooming, and
> enter the cities of Gods.

As Baraka becomes more resolved in his role as poet-priest ("Muslim soothsayer,"[19] as he put it in a 1969 interview), his poetry shows a corresponding tranquility, a calmness which all too frequently deteriorates into prosaic vapidity. Although the writer's healing intentions may be admirable, such intentions do not necessarily constitute poetry. This is especially the case in those works which require no imaginative response from the reader, *i.e.*, those works which tell the message instead of provoking the reader to construct his own responses. This is most glaringly obvious in works without the redeeming intensity of language and dramatic situation of works previously discussed. Note the following questions from "Cold Term."

> Why cant we love each other and be beautiful?
> Why do the beautiful corner each other and spit
> poison? Why do the beautiful not hangout together
> and learn to do away with evil? Why are the beautiful
> not living together and feeling each other's trials?
> Why are the beautiful not walking with their arms around
> each other laughing softly the soft laughter of black beauty?

Such lines are marked by a monotony rarely seen in the previously discussed wroks. "Stirling Street September (for Sylvia)," which appears to have been written shortly after the writer and his second wife took their Arabic names, is characterized by a similar doctrinal flatness:

> I CAN BE THE BEAUTIFUL BLACK MAN
> because I am
> the beautiful black man, and you, girl, child nightlove,
> you are beautiful
> too.
> We are something, the two of us
> the people love us for being
> though they call us out our
> name, [. . .]

At his worst the poet seems to take the postion that the use of certain key words and phrases will excuse even the most insipid writing. Note the instructive lines of "The Calling Together."

> Be somebody Beautiful
> Be Black and Open
> Reach for God
>
>> And succeed
>> in your life world heaven
>> will scream at you
>> to enter, enter Black Man
>> bathe in Blackness

On occasion, the poet, in his efforts to teach the "victims" that they are the last repositories of spirituality, transcends banality. "Part of the Doctrine" is marked by a freshness and intensity too seldom seen in the "spiritual" directives.

> RAISE THE RACE RAISE THE RAYS THE RAZE RAISE IT
> RACE RAISE
> ITSELF RAISE THE RAYS OF THE SUNS RACE TO RAISE IN
> THE RAZE
> OF THIS TIME AND THIS PLACE FOR THE NEXT, AND THE
> NEXT RACE
> OURSELVES TO EMERGE BURNING ALL INERT GASES
> GASSED AT THE
> GOD OF GUARDING THE GUARDIANS OF GOD WHO WE ARE
> GOD IS
> WHO WE RAISE OUR SELVES WHO WE HOVER IN AND ARE
> RAISED
> ABOVE OUR BODIES AND MACHINES THOSE WHO ARE
> WIHOUT GOD
> WHO HAVE LOST THE SPIRITUAL PRINCIPAL OF THEIR
> LIVES ARE
> NOT RAISED . . .
> WE RAISE THE RACE AND THE FACE THROUGH THE EYE OF
> SPACE
> TO RAISE AND THE RAYS OF THE RACE WILL RETURN
> THROUGH ALL SPACE
> TO GOD TO GOD TO GOD TO GOD TO GOD TO GOD TO GOD,
> GOD GOD GOD
> GOD GOD GOD GOD GOD GOD GOD GOD GOD GOD GOD GOD
> GOD GOD GOD GOD
> GOD GOD GOD GODGODGODGODGODGODGODGODGODGOD
> GOD. . . . .

These thunderous and ironic lines (raise the raze) are obviously intended for oral delivery. These lines, too, appear to be lifted from the heart, *i.e.*, the ecstatic climax, of a black fundamentalist sermon. Consider this poem in terms of the following description of the climactic moment of the folk sermon: "With the coming of the spirit, which is the third part of the sermon, the speaker's entire demeanor changes. He now launches into a type of discourse that borders on hysteria. . . . words flow from his lips in such a manner as to make an understanding of them almost impossible."[20] We see a near obliteration of "message" in this poem, with its extensive use of alliteration, internal rhyme, and playful *double Entendre*. The lines themselves seem to aspire to the same spirituality that they seek for the poet's hearers. This aspect is emphasized in the insistent repetition of "GOD," which is pushed past "meaning" here. The poet's attempt to transcend the strictures of language is even more apparent in such works as "Tresspass into Spirit" and "Vowels 2," both of which have been referred to as "Neo-African chants." "Vowels 2" appears to be the poetic rendering of the change effected by the magic of "Part of the Doctrine." Raised by spiritual rays, the poet is:

        Freeeeeeeeeeeeeeeeeeeeeeeeee

        Freeeeeeeeeeeeeeeeeeeeeeeeee

        Freeeeeeeeeeeeeeeeeeeeeeeeee
                    EEE EEE EEE
                    EEE EEE EEE

                    EEE EEE EEE
                    EEE EEE EEE

        Freeeeeeeeeeeeeeeeeeeeeeeeee

                    BURST

        BODYS MOVING
        BODYS MOVING

This freely spaced sound poem, frequently broken with the directive "PREACH" calls to mind the copious directions to Baraka's drama *Slave Ship*, a work characterized more by its collective movement than by dialogue. This obviously experimental effort is, however, incomplete as a poem and has little or no meaning divorced from actual performance. This is true of much of the writer's later poetry. However, in attempting to reach a new audience, Baraka did not completely forsake those elements that brought forth the best of his early work. In much of the late work we still see evidence of poetry written for its visual as well as its auditory effect. The writing of *In Our Terribleness* is proof of this.

    Some of Baraka's best poetry appears in *In Our Terribleness*

(Some elements and meaning in black style), a collection of poems and pictures by Baraka and photographer Fundi (Billy Abernathy). A paean to the vitality, endurance, and distinct style exhibited by the inhabitants of the black inner city, this book is much more than a "most physically pretentious book"[21] in which the poet has "overwritten his point."[22] To be sure, the work has its superfluities, *i.e.*, the "mirror" and the various mystical images and symbols (Clyde Taylor is not too extreme in his humorous assertion that "Some of his symbols look like paraphernalia left over from a Shriner's convention."[23]) Moreover, the book has its patently unpoetic sections. These instances are invariably those in which the poet too heavy-handedly takes it upon himself to "teach Kawaida" and spread the doctrine of Karenga. The following lines, in which the poet lists the seven principles of Karenga's US organization, are exemplary of the recurring didacticism:

> . . . it will be a value system
> that changes us. Something that preaches Unity, Self Determination,
> Collective Responsibility, Collective Economics, Purpose, Creativity,
> and Faith. Faith in Blackness. Changes us to Powerful Beings on the
> planet. Our style will remain.

The same doctrinal flatness creeps into his lines accompanying a picture of the protective force of the Black Muslims, the Fruit of Islam:

> . . . we must organize and be in organization. An organization (FOI
> here
> from the mosque) is the swell of next level consciousness.
> Bigger than the individual. We move from the single to the many
> to the larger the city. the nation. And then past these we move
> to many nations, as one, as Nkrumah and Garvey envision, the many
> blacks into the One Huge Black Nation. . . .

As evidenced in these lines, Baraka, at this stage of his career, is completely dedicated to the principles of black nationalism. No longer merely interested in cultural nationalism, the poet, like the Pan-Africanists he mentions, desires the actual establishment of a black-owned-and-governed territory. The remarkable thing about this book, perhaps, is that the writer manages to get so much poetry in between the political and religious dogma. He does it, moreover, with an abundance of wit and extensive use of the black idiom, which is poetry itself.

The poet announces early in the text that *In Our Terribleness* is an exploration of the black idiom and manner. In language fraught with double meaning, he tells us to watch not only the "pitchas" but the words as well, for,

> They are de signs.
> And the kidz is the whole cycle. An old man looks one way
> (dig it, the language) and old man *looks one way*—his yng son
> *looks another.*

After warning the reader that he is concerned with the magical powers of the word, the poet goes on to explain the particularly black and inverted meaning implied in the book's title. "Our terribleness" translates roughly "our unmatched excellence" (Poet Sonya Sanchez uses the idiom in a similar manner in her title *We a Baaddd People*). Baraka explains the meaning of "bad" by way of exemplary statements and the assertion that blacks literally do speak a different language:

> Since there is a "good" we know is bullshit, corny as Lawrence
> Welk on Venus, we will not be that hominy shit. We will be,
> definitely, bad, bad, as a mother-fucker.
> "That's a bad vine that dude go on."
> "Damn."
> "Its a bad dude."

Just as he contrasts the spoken idiom of the black American to that of the dominant culture—"That's a bad vine that dude got on" translates "That's a beautiful suit the gentleman is wearing"—he constantly juxtaposes other black styles (*e.g.*, musical, or athletic) to middle American styles. In the poet's mind, Lawrence Welk is the musical personification of a stilted dominant culture, whereas John Coltrane, Duke Ellington, and Sun Ra are the vibrant representatives of the black American. They are "terrible" musicians.

> To be bad is one level
> But to be terrible, is to be
> badder dan nat

Preceding the pictures themselves, the poet explains the "functional" nature of the work. In this explanation, Baraka praises the genius of his co-creator, Billy Abernathy, and simultaneously describes what he conceives to be the essence of the artistic process:

> In our terribleness. We wanted to
> conjur with Black Life to recreate it for our selves. So that
> the connection with you would be a bigger Self. Abernathy has
> many many photos each "bad" in some aspect. Abernathy is himself,
> a terrible terbul dude. The way the terribleness of us get thru
> thru him to us, again. The artist completing the cycle recreating.

As these lines demonstrate, the poet is still very much a product of his background. This is evidenced in the swift transition to the sophisticated language of the academician. The poet has rejected some of his earlier fundamental assumptions, however. A comparison of these lines and "Green Lantern's Solo" exemplifies the most basic change. We recall that "Green Lantern's Solo" was a scathing indictment of the closed circle of Village poets. Their works, conceived in a sheltered milieu and imparted to the same, had lost meaning. We see, in the poet's "explanation" of *In Our Terribleness*, Baraka's artistic ideal. Like Abernathy, the real artist distills the essential truth of a larger life and gives it back in an accessible and humanizing form.

The doctrinal thrust of *In Our Terribleness* is like that of much of the poetry discussed in the earlier pages of this chapter. The poet is primarily concerned with mending the black American's shattered sense of self. In this work Baraka attempts to bring out the spiritual beauty just in back of the so-often depraved facade of the "blood's," *i.e.*, black man's, reality.

> Som ter-bul dudes. The glimpse of reality. Not simple fact, which
> is the object trying to talk. But truth. The settling beneath
> appearance to what is shining like the hot beautiful holy sun,
> So the blood. Whatever we say. Always talk so bad about the blood
> "The blood aint ready. A nigger aint shit. Negroes aint go no
> values. Man, these spooks'll make you tired, with they shit." And
> on and on. Trapping ourselves in screens of negative description.
> When we know we bad. Shit, we here. We here and gonna survive.

One wonders, in just how many black barber shops, pool halls, and barrooms did the poet sit, and for how long? The speech is just that authentic. Moreover, the poet seems to draw very deliberately on those elements traditionally accepted as "poetic," just to show that he is equal to the task. The poem itself is an effective example of the extended metaphor. Aside from the striking simile of the third line and the metaphor of the seventh, the whole is enriched by striking uses of incremental repetition, assonance and consonance, particularly in lines three and four.

In the long poem "Prayer for Saving," Baraka introduces his pervasive concern with black heritage, the theme that has grown progressively stronger is works from *The Dead Lecturer* on. He pleads:

> let our words and music survive
> let the temptations please let their feeling survive
> Please Black People Defend John Coltrane and Sun Ra
> Claude McKay must survive his long black Knowledge walks
> in footprint sands of europe america and west indies must stand
> his banana boats and homes in harlem must be protected at all costs
> and Duke Ellington we must hear him in the 22nd century as
> sweetly and the flying images of sound enlightenment his
> diminuendos and crescendos must be preserved behind the alleyways
> and broken stoops of Howard Street and Centre Street [. . .]

Not only are the musical allusions black. The literary allusions are also in the latter works. Recall "The Mighty Flight." Claude McKay is remembered, of course, for his influence on the so-called Harlem Renaissance, the race-conscious literary movement of the 1920's. Ellington is praised for his general excellence as well as his race-conscious music. Speaking of Ellington, Baraka has said: ". . . there have always been musicians who have been deeply conscious of their exact placement in the social world, or at least there was a kind of race pride or consciousness that animated the musicians and their music (. . . here, Ellington is a giant. 'Black Beauty,' 'Black, Brown, and Beige,' 'For My People' and so many many others)." Elsewhere he has spoken of the *avant garde* musician Sun Ra and Ellington in the same context: "Ra's music changes places, like Duke's 'jungle music.' Duke took people to a spiritual past, Ra to a spiritual future. . . ."[24] "Prayer for Saving" is undoubtedly one of the writer's performance poems, as evidenced by the Whitmanesque cataloguing, which allows for relative ease of comprehension on the part of the listeners. It is evident also in the poem's humor, always an advantage to the oral

poet. The black audience would not fail to see the humor in the
poet's reference to the urban hipster's insatiable appetite for extrava-
gant, flashy, or what some would call "loud," clothing:

> defend the energy the hipness in you
> its too valuable that people everywhere understand
> why we got so many dances
> why we like colors
> [. . .]
> > Survive
> > and Defend
> > Survive
> > and Defend
> suedes and maroon pants

This same humor is seen in the poet's accompanying lines to
Abernathy's picture of Willie Waller, a switchblade-carrying street
hipster, dressed in a leather and suede jacket and alligator shoes.
Speaking simultaneously of Willies's dreams and his flair for the re-
splendent, the poet says:

> When he get a shoe factory willie waller
> from howard street shoes might have lights on the
> > motherfuckers.

Baraka ignores no facet of style or "badness" as manifested by
the black urban hipster. In cinematographic swiftness, he lauds
basketball players, hip walkers (limpers), scat singers. They all display:

> That consciousness. Dudes that can
> hang in the air, double up, stuff!! or hold one arm stiff turning
> the corner Abernathy said "Bop do be do be dillia do be da da do be
> dopp woo daaaaa" If you can dig it This is our expression. This is
> the change. And the language the words will change.

Here the poet intimates a calmer version of his revolutionary vision.
He seems to reject, at least momentarily, the grim forcast seen in *The
Slave*. To be sure, the West will fall. It will fall, however, to the
subtly-conquering black style. The poet already sees evidence of the

change, and he speaks humorously of it. He *hears* the change taking place:

> All
> our terribleness is our total. Our hipness is in anything we touch.
> (Wow the weatherman's talking like a nigger. Damn the MC sound
>   like
> a junkie.

Baraka speaks of the powerfully infectious nature of black life in a manner quite similar to that of satirist Ishmael Reed. Reed, too, is concerned with the vibrant spiritualizing force of the Afro-American style. In his *Mumbo Jumbo*, Reed mythicizes this life force in the "Jes Grew" plague, dreaded by anti-spiritual forces led by the "Wallflower Order." Reed compares the unconquerable "Jes Grew" plague to negative epidemics in the following manner: "Some plagues arise from decomposing animals but Jes Grew is electric as life and is characterized by ebullience and the delight of the gods."[25] *In Our Terribleness* is Baraka's testment to the potency of Jes Grew and the "bloods" who, in spite of all, refuse to disavow it.

Although much of the writing of this book appears to be poorly coordinated with the pictures, there is an occasionally perfect pairing. In such cases the totality of effect is overwhelming. A particularly striking instance is seen in the treatment of the aproned, toothpick-chewing laborer. In lines that emphasize the dramatic reversal of the poet's earliest thought (recall "Notes for a Speech," page *25*), Baraka speaks of this contemporary black urban worker in terms of his residual Africanness, no matter the worker's physical placement in the world:

> The blood is the nation in its entirety. What's pictured here is
> our nation.
> Like this blood with the tooth pick. Can you put a Kafiyah on him
> where he stands. Mchawi a wizard they could all be wizards. They
> could and are. The toothpick spraying it around. The touch of light.
> Transformed wood. A wand. Transmutation. The dumb wood now
> vibrating at a higher rate. With the blood. His mouth wand.
> The toothpick of the blood is his casual swagger stick. Sho
> is hip.
> Catches the light

in the steel town
catches a dancers
eye. A smile like a city
laugh
years later
of hard
sunlight

These powerful lines, too, are concerned with "the settling beneath
to what is shining like the hot beautiful holy sun. . . ." Baraka has
rarely employed imagery more precisely. He is again very consciously
"poetic" in these lines. The movement of the poem is highly reminiscent of the characteristic Romantic poem of imaginative transcendence. Like the speaker of Coleridge's "Eolian Harp" or "This Lime
Tree Bower," the speaker of this poem moves, by observable grada-
tion, from the manifested world to a spiritual or visionary awareness. This movement is expressed by the rhythm as well as the
diction of the poem. We notice a movement from the long, prosaic,
earthbound lines of the introduction to the shorter and, finally,
ecstatic staccato bursts of lines six and seven. The poet's conscious
manipulation of sound effects makes this movement even more
striking. The persistent repetition of the word "blood," with all its
associated meanings, and the marked employment of consonance
produce a magic suggested in the wording itself. The height of the
visionary experience—the perception of the other-worldly nature of
the "blood"—is signalled in the move to more lyrical lines.

     Like the suggestive rhythmic progression, the transcendent
state is reflected in the magical effect of such terms as the Swahili
"Mchawi" (sorcerer), "wizard," "transformed," "wand," and "Trans-
mutation." Also as in the Romantic poem, this speaker rebounds
heavily to the commonplace world. The intrusion of this world is
presented in the form of the question asked by an insensitive boor,
who surely represents the dominant culture at its worst. Following
the music of the preceding lines, the question has a shattering effect:

(Hey whydo youse carry that in your mout' Kookie fangblood asked)

This voice is the enemy of the spirit. Not only does he deny the poet
his vision, he also denies the "blood" his right to *be*, *i.e.*, to live

according to his own dictates, his own sense of style. The brusque
intrusion does not completely invalidate the poet's vision, however.
He salvages enough of it to conclude:

> This is the core. The music under the skin. Of the blood. The way we
> walk is a relation to our majesty. The way we hump under shadders.
> The blood. Worship us because we close to god. This man got a tooth
> pick. Yeh. Can you dig it??

An expression of his passionate love for the supposed "dregs"
of our society, *In Our Terribleness* is often exemplary of the poet's
latter tactic of overcompensation. Although this strategy leaves him
open to charges of reverse racism, he is convinced that the "victims,"
conditioned to look on themselves as evil incarnate— "trapping
[themselves] in screen of negative description"—must be forced into
the recognition of their own divinity. Corollary to this is the author's
increasing presentation of the white man as the embodiment of evil.
This idea is given ritualistic form in the play *A Black Mass*. Again the
poet attempts to justify such extreme and simplistic myth-making in
terms of his desired end, *i.e.*, the psychological emancipation of the
black man, who, while looking on himself as evil incarnate, all too
often accepted without question the omnipotence of his oppressors.
As stated earlier, however, this extremely handsome book repeatedly escapes the limitations of such proselytizing, and in so doing, it
bears testament to the poet's power. At its more successful moments
it synthesizes the very best elements of the preceding work.

*Experimental Death Unit #1, Madheart, Great Goodness of Life, A
Black Mass*, and *Slave Ship*

In explaining his decision to abandon the novel form, dramatist Ed Bullins undoubtedly expresses the sentiment of poet-play-
wright-novelist LeRoi Jones—both writers in search of the black
audience. Bullins says: "I was busting my head trying to write novels
and felt somehow that my people don't read novels. . . . But when
they are in the theatre, then I've got them. Or like TV. You know,

my ideas can get to them. So, I moved away from prose forms and into theatre.

. . . now in the theatre, we can go right into the Black community and have a literature for the people, for the 'people-people,' . . . for the great masses of Black people."²⁶ It was this same feeling that forced Baraka to reconsider his role as dramatist. Although, as noted earlier, he did not abandon his poetic effects, he did attempt to reconcile them with his new oral, and doctrinal, priorities. His drama manifests a similar reorientation.

The latter plays, *i.e.*, those written after *The Slave*, are most notably characterized by their overt didacticism. Like the medieval artist Baraka shows in his later drama an unswerving dedication to the pedagogical uses of art. He, too, takes the position that art must, above all, be concerned with moral truth. Moreover, Baraka believed, as did Thomas Hooker and American Puritan "aestheticians," that this moral truth must be presented in a simple manner, a manner "to direct the apprehension of the meanest."²⁷ Baraka very consciously employs the allegorical-didactic technique of medieval drama in much of the work to be considered here.

Like the latter poems, these plays are centrally concerned with (1) identifying and destroying those forces that would exterminate the black man, and (2) inspiring the black man with a renewed sense of self. In the tradition of agit-prop theater, most of these works are tremendously concentrated provocations to action. Consequently, the complexities observed in the earlier works (especially complexity or character) are generally sacrificed in favor of simplicity, explicitness, and brevity. The works to be considered here are consummate examples of modern black agit-prop, or "street theatre," as it is more commonly called by its creators. In his "Short Statement on Street Theatre," Ed Bullins characterizes the genre:

> Street Theatre is the name given to the play or dramatic piece (*i.e.*, skit, morality or political farce or black "commercial" that subliminally broadcasts blackness) written expressly to be presented upon the urban streets and adapted to that purpose. . . .
>
> 1.   Purpose: communicating to masses of Black people . . . who would not ordinarily come or be drawn into the theatre. . . .

3. Types of plays: short, sharp, incisive plays are best. Contemporary
    themes, satirical pieces on current counter-revolutionary figures or
    enemies of the people, humorous themes, also children's plays with
    revolutionary lessons are good street play material. Also, startling
    unique material, something that gives the masses identifying images,
    symbols and challenging situations. Each individual in the crowd
    should have his sense of reality confronted, his consciousness
    assaulted.[28]

With the exception of the child's play,the five plays to be discussed here manifest elements of each type cited by Bullins. "Count-
er-revolutionary figures" repeatedly bear the brunt of the dramatist's
criticism, and although none of these works are wholly humorous, at
least not intentionally so, they are all spiced with the comic. In Baraka's *Jello*, however, a burlesque of the Jack Benny—Rochester relationship, we see pure farce. This work is interesting in that it is additional evidence of the artist's changing frame of reference. In *Jello*,
as in other late works, he returns to pop-cult material but with a
complete reversal of attitude. What was once "high camp" and representative of a lost innocence is dismissed in this re-creation of the
Jack Benny Show. Baraka's humorously "revolutionary" Rochester
represents, of course, the rebellious instinct lurking within the most
ostensibly passive black man; *i.e.*, Rochester, too, is brother to Clay.
All the works to be discussed in this chapter, particularly *A Black
Mass* and *Slave Ship*, attempt to give the viewers "identifying images,
symbols and challenging situations."

According to dates given in *Four Black Revolutionary Plays*,
Experimental Death Unit #1 was written in 1964 and first performed on March 1, 1965, at St. Mark's Playhouse, New York city. This
work is obviously a product of what I have referred to as the writer's
"middle passage," *i.e.*, the phase discussed in Chapter II. The basic
theme of anti-art and the prevailing censure of those the writer calls
"liberals" are both still present in this play, but now muted in comparison to earlier treatments. Both of these former concerns are over-
whelmed by the urgent call to black unity and pride. This shift in
message is accompanied by a marked shift in method. The dramatist
forsakes the strict naturalism of *The Toilet* and its corollary examina-
tions of character and motive. He also abandons the more complex
symbolic techniques of *Dutchman* and *The Slave*, and replaces them
with a much simpler format. This latter development can be seen in

terms of the conventions of the medieval stage. This analogy is all the more plausible in light of Baraka's description of the later *Madheart* as "a morality play."

As in the morality play, the forces of good and evil are starkly contrasted in the latter plays of Baraka. However, the agit-prop artist makes certain crucial changes in adapting the medieval play for 20th Century black nationalist use. Instead of vying for the soul of "Every man," the forces of vice and virtue do battle for the soul of "Black Man." Moreover, vice is invariably personified by white characters or black characters who display intense hatred for themselves. Virtue is represented by blacks who throw off any force that tends to limit their full human growth, freedom, and self-reliance. The dichotomy is often underscored through the use of masks.

Baraka demonstrates the pervasiveness of the medieval influence in the opening dialogue of *Experimental Death Unit*. In what seems to be simply another example of the semantically "right," but essentially nonsensical, exchanges of the absurdists, we observe what is acutally an example of the old literary debate so often used by homiletic writers. Like the Owl and the Nightingale of medieval debate, Duff and Loco posit two diametrically opposed world views. In this case, however, the differences are finally only superficial. In acknowledging their apparent differences, Duff pointedly alludes to this earlier debate:

> DUFF: Your're unlike the nightingale, a sob sister. . .
>   a helpmate to the weak.

The opening dialogue enhances the static quality of the characters. Because of the mechanical nature of their utterances, we are almost immediately aware of the speakers as icons or near-abstractions. (The same is true of the "virtuous" young automatons of the play's conclusion). Although Duff is not called "Greed" or "Ego," his first statements bludgeon us into the awareness that he is the personification of these vices. In like manner, Loco's first remarks force upon us an understanding of his stilted role. A guilt-ridden hipster, Loco is as much an ethical type as Duff. His later actions are evidence of his kinship to Lula and those generally characterized as "liberals" by the dramatist. I will discuss the allegorical implications of these characters later.

Loco is different from the earlier portrayal of the liberal in that he is not allied with the aesthetes. In fact, he has only scorn for them. His comments mirror those of his creator:

> LOCO: I despise beauty. What you mean by that.
> I hate these fools who walk around and call
> themselves artists, whose sole connection
> with anything meaningful is the alcohol decay
> of their skins. Weak dope dripping out of
> their silky little beards.

To emphasize the point, Baraka uses the utterly repugnant Duff to speak in behalf of artists. Duff's "defense" is a blatantly ironic corroboration of the dramatist's fundamental criticism of the Western artist:

> DUFF: They (artists) are necessary for the world to
> continue.

Although the opening dialogue is sprinkled with just enough "meaning" to assure a "street" audience's comprehension of Duff and Loco as types, their bizarre banter is undoubtedly meant to alienate that same audience. Their strange language is intended to emphasize their "otherness." This is all the more plausible in light of the contrasting first statement of the black woman. Through her earthy comments, the author seeks to achieve the opposite effect. He attempts to force the black audience to acknowledge kinship with her. She speaks the language of the streets. Note her greeting:

> WOMAN: Ho boys [. . .] Hey bararebop . . . two sports.

She knows that the best rebuttal to a personal affront must be expressed in terms of the dozens. She tells Duff:

> You lick your mother's neck! [. . .] But lick mine too. In this
> terrible charlieland.

Here reference to America as "charlieland" shows, moreover, her understanding of and creative manipulation of black slang. In black slang, "Mr. Charlie" is, of course, the generic term for the white man. In these and other such statements, Baraka asserts the essential humanity of this tragic woman, who, according to the stage directions, *"could probably have been an attractive woman, in another life. About forty, still gallantly seductive."* Trapped between the ritualized vices of Loco and Duff and the equally rigid virtues of the young black revolutionaries at the play's end, she is the play's most calculated concession to "realism." By presenting her in such a manner, the moralizing dramatist obviously sought to make her example more moving.

Aside from the more general implications of their static roles, Duff and Loco are perhaps best understood in terms of the two distinct categories discussed by Baraka in the essay "What Does Nonviolence Mean?" Written in 1963, only a year of so before *Experimental Death Unit*, this particular essay goes far in explaining the symbolic purport of both characters. Speaking of the "war" against racial oppression, Baraka says:

> So far the most serious battles in the war I spoke of are being waged between two classes of white men, although the middle-class Negroes are the semi-conscious pawns in these struggles (The rest of the black population are pawns by default). The battles are being waged now, have been waged for the last three hundred years, between those white men who think the Negro is good for one thing and those who think he is good for another. This same fight went on during the early days of slavery between the missionaries, those who would give the slave Christianity, thereby excusing the instance of slavery as a moral crusade (with concomitant economic advantages) and those who felt that as animals they had no soul. The fight continues today, with the same emphasis . . . the war goes on, from battle to battle, but with essentially the same things at stake, and for the same reasons. The forces of naked repression, on the one hand, have always been out in the open. What they want, have wanted, is common knowledge to Negroes once Negroes have gotten old enough to find out that the world is basically unfriendly if you are black. Each "class" (of white people) has its own method of making that world unfriendly, which makes the quarrel. But nothing is really to be changed. Complete socio-economic subjugation is the goal of both white forces. What the liberal sees as evil about this program is the way it is being carried out. Liberals want to be leaders rather than rulers.[29]

With this statement in mind, it is extremely difficult to ignore the allegorical implications of *Experimantal Death Unit*. Indeed, both men, Duff and Loco, want to "screw" the black woman. They differ only in their approaches. Duff clearly represents "the forces of naked repression." His earliest lines convince us of the correctness of this reading.

> DUFF: Well, sufferer, my windows are as icy as the rest
>   of the world.
>   [...]
>   I'm as sacred as anyone, and I say the world is
>   to the man who will take it.

Moreover, he looks upon the woman as animal:

> [...] All those holes in your body I want to fill. I got meat and mind
> to do it with. I mean out there in the street. I'll throw you down . . .
> mount you, giddyap! giddyap! big-assed nigger lady! . . . then I ride you
> right out through the rain [. . .]

Loco, however, expresses his desire to use the woman, *i.e.*, to keep her in her degraded role, in more lyrical phrases. Although he is primarily concerned with his own gratification, he shrewdly inverts the terms:

> Consider me a ready youth. Made to be used, under and because of
> you.

He also spouts platitudes as he declares his love:

> Madam, madam . . . I love you . . . I want to roll around with you in
> calm afternoons . . . remember that. But God is (*Pointing*) up there!
> And I believe He knows what's best.

At bottom Loco is concerned only with the uses to which his guilt-ridden psyche can put the black woman. His supplication to her merely serves to bolster the myth of his own moral being. Although there is much truth in his indictment of self, Loco only wants to *feel* moral. He admits as much in demanding, along with Duff, certain comforts from the woman. As he guiltily anticipates possession of her, Loco says:

Yes, if we do it . . . we have a right to feel right too.

To be sure, Baraka approaches this sexual encounter ambivalently. On the one hand, she is clearly the abused black woman who submits to her own misuse. On the other, she is given a vague superiority over the men. This is implied in their groveling before and under her, actions which would present them in a decidedly negative light in the minds of the street audience. Moreover, for metaphorical purposes, the act of cunnilingus is quite suggestive. Duff and Loco seek nourishment from this "still gallantly seductive" woman. They seek life and direction in her residual beauty, a beauty that she herself does not recognize. The woman, as combined victim and tainted earth mother, fails herself, and the men as well. Therefore, Loco does not bear the full weight of Baraka's censure. For that matter, nor does the thoroughly despicable Duff. As are most of the later plays, *Experimental Death Unit* is a pointed attack on the negative elements within the black community itself.

The woman's willingness to be abused by Loco and Duff is all the more reprehensible because she understands the nature of her exploitation. She lets us know this is her mumblings ("this terrible charlieland," *etc.*). Her justifiable rage is apparent in other remarks:

I charge what you owe [. . .] OWE! OWE! (*She grabs at DUFF's balls.*) Everything. What there is to take. (*Laughs*) From what remains of your dwindling stash.

The woman has even imbibed some of the exhortations to racial pride espoused by groups such as the Muslims. This is evident in her allusion to the glories of the ancient black past, which she contrasts to the fancied decadence of the European past. She says:

Ahhh man, the old folks talked about spirits. *The* Spirit! I'll go mystical when I goddam please [. . .] I'll be off somewhere then, thinking about something that would make you mad. What I care about you? Huh . . . your mother and father eat meat with their hands. I saw them old Robin Hood pictures. You can't tell me nothin.

The woman has clearly heard the stirrings of a new day and it is quite apparent that she senses her personal guilt in her own debasement. She refuses, however, to rectify her ways, to act decisively for her own good. This spurned virtue is embodied in the young revolutionaries. Baraka the moralist very consciously makes the climactic scene a matter of choice. If she chooses Duff, she embraces her own exploitation, continued alienation, and death. On the other hand, by heeding the call of the young soldiers, she can commit herself to purpose, unity, and life. We see, however, the tragedy of her error in her condescending attitude toward the soldiers. To her, the young revolutionary leader is "just a soulbrother," *i.e.*, a defeated inhabitant of the ghetto who will accept her depravity as a part of the natural order of things. She believes that she can, by uttering a few hip phrases and proving herself a "soulsister," go on with business as usual. The dramatist uses language with tremendous effect in this, the climactic scene. The woman's earthy street response again underscores her humanity, her "reality" amidst what are essentially abstractions. She maintains:

> ...it's just a soul brother...don't worry. I'll cool everything out [...] Hey y'all...what's happening? [...] Hey, cats, what's to it? [...] what's happening, man ... why you bein' so cool?

As she falls to the juggernaut forces of purgation, the intended viewers, black street people, presumably recognize their kinship with the woman. In the time-honored manner of the didacticist, the dramatist implies, "If you act in this manner, the same fate will befall you." The severity of the purgative action of this play is typical of numerous "black revolutionary" plays. Perhaps it appears in its most austere form in Jimmy Garrett's *And We Own the Night* (a play that takes its title from a poem by Baraka), wherein a young man kills his "reactionary" mother.

Like *Experimental Death Unit, Madheart* partakes of the conventions of the medieval morality play." It begins with the same compression of character that marks the play just discussed. Vice and virtue are starkly contrasted in the figures of Devil Lady and Black Man. Again character is expressed through the dramatist's employment of the debate. The play begins:

DEVIL LADY: You need pain (*coming out of the shadows with neon torch, honky-tonk calliope music*) You need pain, ol'nigger devil, pure pain, to clarify your desire.

BLACK MAN: (*Turns slowly to look at her, raises his arms, straight out parallel to the floor, then swiftly above his head, then wide open in the traditional gesture of peace*) God is not the devil. Rain is not fire nor snow, nor old women dying in hallways.

DEVIL LADY: There is peace.
BLACK MAN: There is no peace.
DEVIL LADY: There is beauty.
BLACK MAN: None that you would know about.
DEVIL LADY: There is horror. There is (*Pause, as if to cry or precipitate a rush of words which do not come*) . . . only horror. Only stupidity. (*Raising to point at her*) Your stale pussy weeps paper roses.

Through her opening words Devil Lady immediately establishes herself as the embodiment of cruelty. This initial impression is enhanced by her appearance. According to Baraka's instructions, she should wear "*an elaborately carved white devil mask*," yet another clue to the dramatist's appropriation of the medieval mode. According to M. D. Anderson, "The radiance of a divine countenance clearly called for something more than a human face, however comely, and gilded masks seem to have been used for the Divinity . . . . There is even more definite evidence that intense evil was represented theatrically by masks."[30] As in *Experimental Death Unit*, this particular personification of evil is given an even more precise societal implication. In her stylized entrance, "*with neon torch*," she is an extremely sinister Miss Liberty.

With so much "evidence" (her words and her prejudicial appearance) stacked against Devil Lady, Black Man (and later, Black Woman) is instantly ensconced as her antithesis. His manner—arms "*wide open in the traditional gesture of peace*"—cues an inherent benevolence. Black Man's first words also emphasize his veracity. By uttering the incontestable—"God is not the Devil. Rain is not fire . . . ."—he is seen at once as the embodiment of truth. In contradicting her, Black Man also reinforces the audience's perception of Devil Lady as the personification of falsehood. The dramatist also shows the pervasiveness of the "Crow Jane" image in the reference of the Devil Lady's genital organs, a reference marked by the more bizarre street employment of metaphor (discussed on page *118*). Although this treacherous image of the white woman as muse of the Western art tradition is evoked again near the play's conclusion:

> Die, you bitch, and drag your mozarts into your nasty hole. Your mozarts stravinskys stupid white sculpture corny paintings death-fiddles all your crawling jive, [. . .]

it is not a major motif. This more complex symbolic use of the white woman, *i.e.*, as embodiment of a social and aesthetic world view is more characteristic of the works considered in the previous chapter. Although the woman is not divested of all larger or cultural symbolism in the latter works, she assumes a markedly more literal meaning. That is, *Madheart* is much closer in meaning to the poem "W. W." than it is to "Crow Jane."

In *Madheart* Baraka exploits his satiric manner, along with his adaptation of the fundamental principles of the morality play. The element of satire is introduced in the treatment of the Mother and Sister, the two characters for whom the forces of good and evil (Black Man and Devil Lady) contend. In creating these comically degenerate characters, the author intends to render his homiletic drama pleasing. The wig-wearing Mother and Sister, like the lost woman of *Experimental Death Unit*, manifest both ignorance and self-loathing. Their case is more pathetic than that of the whore, however. For the whore, even in the rot of her life, despises her degradation and those who contribute to it. On the other hand, Mother and Sister submit completely to Devil Lady and the standards she embodies. The Mother's reactionary inability to comprehend Black Man's and Black Woman's drive to eradicate Devil Lady and her pernicious influence would surely strike the writer's audience as humorous. Baraka draws as much comedy as possible from the Mother's reactionary or "Tommish" remarks:

> What is wrong with niggers, this time? I'm old and I hump along under my wig.

The Mother's rebuttle to Black Man's threat of death gains the same effect:

> What I care? Batman won't love me without my yellowhead daughter. I'm too old for him or Robin. I can't paint soupcans, the junk I find is just junk, my babies stick in they eyes, I'm sick in the big world? [. . .] Fuck both of you stupid-ass niggers . . . You'll never get no light [. . .]

Again the aspects of Americana that were once high "camp" for the young Beat poet are presented in a decadent light. Along with *avant garde* art (Warhol style), comic strip heroes are seen as emblems of a decadent and enslaving power. The satirical treatment of both Mother and Sister climaxes as they thrash about the stage, wigs pulled down over their eyes, with Mother attempting to feed Sister "jest a little bit o' greens . . . flavored with knuckles," now detested images of the slave past.

The dereliction of these women is reflected, moreover, in their speech. It is quite noticeable that the heroines and heroes of Baraka's latter plays speak a language purged of the baudiest street usages. Presumably the black man or woman whose consciousness is raised shuns "low-down" speech. In *Madheart* Black Man's worst utterance is "bullshit." The demure Black Woman's is the humorous coinage "bitchfool." Not so with the two lost sisters, however. The moralizing dramatist intends their "debased" language to reflect their racial consciousness. This idea attains its expressionistic extreme in the fight between the two women. While flailing away at one another, the women scream in unison:

> Fuckingbitch Fuckingbitch Fuckingbitch Fuckingbitch Fuckingbitch
> Fuckingbitch Fuckingbitch Fuckingbitch Fuckingbitch Fuckingbitch
> Fuckingbitch . . .

Although he wants to damn utterly the backslider, Baraka realizes the danger of encouraging a simple self-righteous scorn on the part of his audience. He attempts to counter this possibility with the blatantly direct appeal, another device of the earliest didacticists. Black Man concludes the play acknowledging his and the audience's responsibility to the lost Mother and Sister. His final remarks bind all

his hearers together in the obligatory struggle to resurrect black dignity. Black Man says to Black Woman and the Audience:

> They're my flesh. I'll do what I can . . . We'll both try. All of us, black
> people.

Prior to this remark, Black Man emphasizes the communal, healing
nature of the theatrical assembly by another direct appeal:

> Let the audience think about themselves, and about their lives when
> they leave this happening. This black world of purest possibility [. . .]
> All our lives we want to be alive. We scream for life.

The frequency of such lines evidences the author's growing
concern with the catechitecal uses of theater. The audience is perceived and addressed as a community of believers who share certain
fundamental ideals. BART/S in Harlem, Spirit House in Newark, and
the Black Arts Alliance in San Francisco, all of which Baraka helped
form, were theatrical missions which encouraged a communal spirit.
As in certain extremely dogmatic religious sects, these theatrical
audiences saw themselves as the truly "saved" members of the black
community. This self-satisfaction is apparent in *Madheart*'s coded
allusion to the restorative powers of the Black Arts Alliance, the
group for which the play was written and by which it was first performed. Surely the audiences of the production staged by the Black
Arts Alliance received the following proposal by Black Man with a
feeling of moral rectitude and consanguinity:

> What is this? [. . .] What's all this mouth mouth action? Why don't
> these women act like women should? Why don't they act like Black
> Women? All this silly rapping and screaming on the floor. I should
> turn them over to the Black Arts and get their heads relined.

Like much of Baraka's early drama, *Madheart* is an exorcistic
work but with this difference: whereas the early plays communicate
the author's attempt to expel various forces form *his* own psyche,
Madheart, like all of the latter work, aims at *collective* exorcism. The
thoroughly engaged black dramatist would remove those psychological bonds responsible for the black woman's diseased conviction that
she is beautiful only when she mimics the white woman. He would
also expel those forces that have made it difficult for black men and

women to love and respect one another. Indeed, a major theme of the play is the reestablishment of the black family, which Baraka equates with the unqualified acceptance of the dominance of the male. The play actually climaxes in lines as faithful to traditional Muslim doctrine as they are obviously repulsive to the "liberated" woman. After slapping *and* kissing her into submission, Black Man says to Black Woman:

> You are my woman, now, forever. Black Woman.

She replies:

> I am your woman, and you are the strongest of God. Fill me with your seed. (*They embrace* [...])

Great Goodness of Life (A Coon Show) is also concerned with the Black Man's virile assertion of courage and masculinity. However, it teaches by negative example. More akin to the mother and sister of *Madheart* than he is to Black Man, Court Royal is another of Baraka's many travestied black middle class characters, in the line descending from "Hymn for Lanie Poo." *Great Goodness* conveys essentially the same "message" as *Dutchman*. However, *Great Goodness* demonstrates the urgency of Baraka's need to reach his new audience. This play, too, is characterized by a relatively simple pedagogic thrust, inspired by medieval drama. The motivating factor of *Great Goodness* is a mysterious summoning of the protagonist, Court Royal. Like the protagonist of *Everyman*, he must account for his "misspent" life. Baraka, of course, inverts the traditional pattern. Instead of accounting to a righteous God and his representatives, Court Royal attempts to palliate a power bent on his own destruction. Baraka's conclusion differs markedly also from the optimistic conclusion of *Everyman*. In this thoroughgoing satire the author is concerned only with the salvation of his audience.

Great Goodness not only reveals the author's obvious appropriation of elements of the medieval mode, but certain expressionistic practices as well. Techniques commonly associated with the dramas of Brecht, Jarry, and other modernists are effectively employed here and in other of Baraka's later plays (see *The Death of Malcolm X,*

Home on the Range, and *Police*). *Great Goodness* is performed in the exageratedly non-realistic manner. This particular mode underscores the psychological implications of Court's confusion. The disembodied voices, superimposed screen images, and disturbing sounds all remind us of the author's coninued awareness of theatrical *avant garde*, reflected earlier in *The Baptism*. These elements are also responsible for the decidedly nightmarish quality of *Great Goodness*.

The setting firmly establishes Court in the tradition of his literary progenitor, Uncle Tom. The action takes place *"outside an old log cabin* [. . .] *"* Court's appearance, *"gray but still young looking,"* is also suggestive, but his name affords us the most conclusive key to his character. Court Royal has spent his life humoring whites and suppressing the honest rage seething within his soul. In his summons we see the objective rendering of Court's inner turmoil. In the manner of the medieval moralist, Baraka personifies the warring factions within his protagonist. In Freudian terms, the Voice of the Judge represents Court's superego, whereas the Young Victim represents his shackled id.

The Voice is that part of Court's psyche that binds him to convention. It is the element to which he has timidly submitted all his life. The Voice demands, in the manner of the thoroughly exposed Lula, that all trace of rebellion be throttled. The Voice refers to Court's deeply buried rage in the assertion:

> You are charged
> with shielding a
> wanted criminal
> A murderer.

Court's disavowal of any transgression is expressed in terms fraught with both humor and great racial meaning for the black audience. Without cessation, Court declares:

> Of course I'm not guilty, I work in the Post Office. (*Tries to work up a little humor*) You know me, probably. Didn't you ever see me in the Post Office? I'm a supervisor; you know me. I work at the Post Office. I'm no criminal. I've worked at the Post Office for thirty-five years. I'm a supervisor. There must be some mistake. I've worked at the Post Office for thirty-five years.

Why does Court feel his innocence so definitively proven through the fact of his employment? Baraka's intended audience knows the answer, and this knowledge grows out of a particular conception of the postal worker. This figure, so familiar and significant in :he black community, in all probability affects Baraka's audience as the well-known medieval personifications affected that particular audience. The Post Office has traditionally been a haven for the black worker. Denied general access tc America's colleges and universities until recent years, many talented blacks without degrees found gainful employment in this department of the relatively bias-free federal government. Faced with the Jim Crow hiring policies of the private sector, even those fortunate blacks with college degrees frequently sought refuge in the Post Office. The Post Office is consequently regarded, with intense ambivalence in the black community, as both a haven and a trap. Because it so often circumscribed aspirations, it has been called the "graveyard of black talent." Too often the black postal worker ignored the stultifying aspects of his employment. In his mania to join the dominant culture, he overlooked the odious roots of his prosperity. Court Royal forgets the compromise inherent in his dilemma.

All the "characters" of *Great Goodness* in some way represent Court Royal's psyche. John Breck, his automaton of a lawyer, is an exaggerated version of the protagonist. The early intimations of Uncle Tom give way to explicit statement in the dramatist's expressionistic description of Breck:

> (*A bald-headed smiling house slave in a wrinkled dirty tuxedo crawls across the stage; he has wire attached to his back leading offstage. A huge key in the side of his head. We hear the motors "animating" his body groaning like tremendous weights. He grins and slobbers, turning his head slowly from side to side. He grins. He makes little quivering sounds.)*

Attorney Breck, a *"middle aged Negro man,"* is also a powerless dupe. Yet he is filled with a false sense of importance. Note his parting comment to Court: "ain't I a bitch . . . I mean ain't I?" In advising Court to admit his guilt, Breck is actually urging him to put down his true rebel self and conform. This is not at all what the Young Victim means when he tells Court to admit his guilt. To make sure that the viewer realizes the kinship of Court and Breck, the dramatist later ascribes a similarly ritualized behavior to Court himself. In the midst of his inquisition, Court performs a machinelike dance strikingly reminiscent of Tod Clifton's "jigaboo" dolls in *Invisible Man*. Court's

> *head jerks like he's suddenly heard Albert Ayler. It raises, his whole body jerks around like suddenly animated ragdoll. He does a weird dance like a marionette jiggling and waggling.*

Court's hatred for black people, his cultural shame, is also given objective treatment in the hooded or *"KKK-like figures"* of the play. His contempt for the abused black woman even surpasses that of the hooded figures. In his mania for "respectability," Court has lost all compassion and cannot appreciate those factors which have brought the "nigger lady" to her degraded pass. He says of her:

> [. . .] She drinks and stinks and brings our whole race down.
>
> HOOD 2: Ain't it the truth!

The Voice, John Breck, and the Hoods all represent one side of Court Royal's psyche. The Young Victim, Court's son, is the objective rendering of the other, the turbulent side of his consciousness. As such, he directly conflicts with the other forces. Recall the Voice's consternation on first hearing the rebellious Young Victim speak. In an attempt to silence him, the Voice panics:

> Get that criminal out of here. Beat him. Shut him up. Get him. *(Now sounds of scuffling come out of darkness. Screams. Of a group of men subduing another man.)*

The darkness is extremely suggestive of the mind of the protagonist. The defiant impulse must be violently forced back into the underbrush of the psyche. If this is not possible, it must be killed. And this is precisely what happens. On orders from the Voice and aided by the Hoods, Court Royal executes the murderer he has harbored in his heart. This final act assumes additional effect, especially for the more literal-minded viewer, in the presentation of the Victim as

Court's son. In light of the tremendous importance Baraka ascribes to parental duty (recall "A Contract....," "Black People," and "Leroy"), Court, on the literal level, commits the ultimate crime.

Of course, one of the play's merits is that it *does* work on the literal level. Needless to say, the "street" audience would hardly appreciate the full psychological implications of the drama. Nevertheless, none of the "edifying" and little of the purely theatrical effect is lost in the more literal reading. Baraka ensures this by employing such intensely meaningful types as Court and the KKK-figures, both calculated to evoke emotionally charged reactions among his viewers. Even the *avant garde* devices are designed with the purely emotional response of the audience in mind. The projections, for example, are not used to "alienate" the audience from the action of the drama (*i.e.*, in the manner of Brecht). Rather, Baraka knows that screen images of slain and abused black heroes—"*Malcolm. Patrice. Rev. King. Garvey. Dead nigger kids killed by the police. Medgar Evers.*"—will elicit a gut response in his intended viewers. These projections make Court Royal's guilt more real, hence more despicable. Because of the author's skilled intermixture of the real and the surreal, *Great Goodness* is one of the few of Baraka's latter works to roughly approximate the power of *Dutchman*, distinguished by this same skillful admixture.

Baraka appropriates elements from not only the medieval morality play in the creation of his later works; he also adapts the medieval mystery play to his design. The writers of the mysteries presented religious subjects—saints' lives, biblical stories, apocryphal material—in dramatic form for their largely unlettered audiences. As Anderson assesses their significance: "In an age when few of the laity could read, various forms of spoken drama played an important part in their religious instruction. Long before the first plays were performed, dramatic elements had been introduced into the ritual of the Church, and later medieval congregations were made familiar, through sermons and readings from vernacular texts, with those lively apocrypal expansions of the Scriptures, the legends of the saints and moral allegories, which were the raw material of the first English playwrights."[31] *A Black Mass* is the striking instance of Baraka's utilization of the mystery writer's *modus operandi*. In spite of the drama's professed seriousness, we immediately recognize the drama-tist's conscious amusement, in the manner of Ishmael Reed, at the expense of medieval dramatic convention. The "orthodoxy" he chooses to dramatize for the benefit of his illiterate laity is Elijah Muhammad's myth of Yacub, the story of the man who, "embittered toward Allah . . . , decided, as revenge, to create upon the earth a devil race—a bleached-out, white race of people."[32] This malignant myth is discussed at length in *The Autobiography of Malcolm X.*

Like the later poems of Baraka, *A Black Mass* is characterized by a decidedly mystical, empyreal aura. Meant to inspire black men to reclaim their original virtue, this tone is suggested in the author's earliest directives. The scene is described: *"Jet blackness, with may-be a blue or red-violet glow. Soft peacful music (Sun-Ra). Music of eternal concentration and wisdom."* This tone is reinforced through the majestic dress (*"long exquisite robes"*) of the characters and the employment of traditional Muslim names. Finally, the elaborate set-ting suggests an other-wordliness at odds with the typically spare backdrop of the agit-prop play. The action takes place against *"The outline of some fantastic chemical laboratory . . . with weird mix-tures bubbling, colored solutions (or solutions that glow in the dark)."* All of these elements suggest the once-sanctified lives of the ancestors of the now-debased black man.

As in *Madheart*, Baraka attempts to sustain the ennobling aura through ornate language and stylized performance. The characters speak an exaggeratedly stilted idiom, completely purged of the crack-ling profanities that enlivened the earlier poems and plays. Frequent-ly the dialogue for *A Black Mass* reminds us of the formality of Greek drama. This is especially true of the women's chorus-like re-porting of off-stage calamity:

EULALIE: The elements disturb us, Lord Magician. The elements
             threaten us.
OLABUMI: The sky is not the sky. The earth trembles beneath our
             feet.

TILA: The sea shudders and rages, and throws strange creatures
             on the land.

On occasion they exclaim in unison:

Ooooh . . . The earth is alien. Our mothers are sick, the world has shrunk and is choking us.

The magicians, too, frequently speak in the exalted manner. Note Tanzil's apprehensive remark:

Jacoub, I fear we teeter above the horrible void.

No doubt Baraka is consciously, perhaps humorously, employing the conventions of Greek drama in this, his appropriation of the medieval mystery play. It is most apparent in his use of the women, who, in maintaining a mood music of sorts, encourage the audience to feel along with the players. This markedly "choral" function is quite literally manifest in the women's final lament, rendered after Tanzil's request:

TANZIL: Sing, women. Sing against this madness and evil. Jacoub.
             Let the women create their gentle thing here, their rich
             life smells. Sing, women. Against this sucking death we
             see. Sing. (*The women, pulling themselves close to
             each other, huddled in their fear, raise their voices, at
             first very softly, with the purring of beautiful pussies.
             Then they begin to shriek their songs (Sun-Ra songs),
             as if in terror against the two white shivering things
             quivering in the middle of the laboratory.*)

The dominant themes of *A Black Mass* are those that have possessed the writer's mind from *The Dead Lecturer* on. In *A Black Mass*, we see, however, the first complete dramatization of these obsessive ideas. Even more than does his beastly white creation, Jacoub, the black scientist, bears the dramatist's censure. It is Jacoub who, in the manner of the writer's former associates, seeks to dissociate thought and feeling and who strives to flatter his own ego by creating for its own sake. In opposition to his brother magicians, who live contentedly in harmony with the universe, exhibiting a cosmic consciousness (exemplified in their appropriation of the modern street phrase, "Everything is Everything"), Jacoub, who has already invented the evil of time, asserts that "creation is its own end." In a statement which proves conclusively that these are early concerns treated anew in a *A Black Mass*, Baraka has humorously asserted in one essay, "Yacub [the Black Muslim spelling] was first of all a new critic . . ."[33] To be sure, Baraka's ghetto audience does not comprehend the nature of the dramatist's continuing argument with his former associates. Consequently, this intellectual-aesthetic argument is deliberately deemphasized. The graphic rendering of the "beast's" creation clearly reaches out to the literal-minded and emotionally-oriented audience.

As stated earlier, Baraka attempts to justify his simplistic equation of good with blackness and evil with whiteness on the grounds of necessary over-compensation. Baraka specifically implies this motivation in his creation of *A Black Mass* with the following denial of the charge of racism: "Racism is a theory, as life motif, of why something is inferior, check out Tacitus and 'The Teutonic Origins' theory of white first, with the rest of life sloping off xenophobically down the scale to bad us. We are not racists, when we accuse white people, it is based on still observable phenomena."[34] *A Black Mass* is Baraka's pedagogic and concrete rebuttal to the aforementioned "theory."

The tone of ritualistic exorcism works with the author's increasing efforts to induce audience involvement in *A Black Mass*. The audience is urged to acknowledge the very real presence of the "beast" in the world by the author's directions, directions which present the black man's peril in most palpable form. Jacoub's evil creation and the now-contaminated Tiila *"howl and hop, and then, turning to the audience, their mouths drooling and making obscene gestures, they move out into the audience, kissing and licking people as they hop eerily out, still screaming: "White! Me . . . Me . . . Me . . . Me . . . White!"* This final scene is followed by the parting words of a heretofore unheard "Narrator," whose appeal to unity reminds us of Black Man's in *Madheart*. He invokes:

And so Brothers and Sisters, these beasts are still loose in the world, still they spit their hideous cries. There are beasts in our world, Brothers and Sisters. There are beasts in the world. Let us find them and slay them. Let us lock them in their caves. Let us declare the Holy War. The Jihad. Or we cannot deserve to live. Izm-el-Azam.

Izm-el-Azam. Izm-el-Azam. Izm-el-Azam. (*Repeated until all lights*
black)

Roland Reed points out that *A Black Mass* is a conscious
appropriation of certain elements of the Catholic Mass. He says of
the Narrator's concluding charge, "There is certainly in the final
speech of the Narrator a parallel with the final blessing of the Catholic Mass, '*Ite Missa est*, Go, the Mass is, it exists, it continues' (Christians Around the Altar. 74). Like the Catholic Mass, Baraka's play
implies a strong missionary commitment."[35] In this play as a whole
and the final charge in particular, the dramatist seeks to foster in his
audience both a sense of shared peril and an awareness of collective
responsibility. These concerns are epitomized in the "historical
pageant" *Slave Ship*.

In *Slave Ship*, first produced in 1969, Baraka demonstrates his
continuing awareness of the newest theatrical modes. This play is a
consummate example of the "living" or "environmental" theater of
the 1960's. Unlike the plays of the conventional stage, environmental
theater seeks, above all, to produce in the audience a sense of community. In the words of one critic, "The message of the new environmental theater was: 'Come together!' "[36] In their desire to bring
about this end, the creators of this radical theater do all in their power to convince their audiences that they are an integral part of the
drama. Given Baraka's increasingly priestly bearing, his theatrical
efforts were inevitably headed in this particular direction.

Richard Schechner, former editor of *The Drama Review* and
the foremost spokesman for environmental theater, defines this
theater in terms of its energetic movement. Instead of the traditional
explicitly delineated *action*, the audience is confronted with a markedly more engrossing *activity*. One need only read *Slave Ship* to begin to appreciate this distinction. Of course, an actual witnessing of
this dramatic "event" (another word dear to Schechner) provides
even more conclusive evidence of Baraka's employment of the
fundamental tenets of the environmentalists.

Of particular interest is the author's use of space, one of the
most important aspects of environmental theater. In *Slave Ship*,
Baraka exploits the spatial element by opening up the traditional

"playing area" into the usual terrain of the spectators. The audience feels oneness with the players not merely through their various overtures (culminating in the commual dance at the end of the play), but also because Baraka's ingenious set "involves" the audience from the start of the drama. The effect of this total re-creation of the environment is described by one witness of the first New York showing of the play:

> The set itself, a split-level wooden platform mounted on huge springs, was a brilliant conception and the play's chief metaphor, suggesting with its rhythmic rocking not simply the swell of the ocean as the slave ship sails across it, but the structural insecurity of the black man both as a slave on his way to America and as a citizen once he has arrived and settled . . . The lower level of the set, the dark hold . . . forced the audience to hunch over in order to see what was happening during the first part of the play.[37]

In this way, the dramatist *forces* the audience to relive the anguish of the "middle passage." The viewer-participants, as they should be called, and the cramped slaves experience a similar discomfort. Just as he sought to make "real" the history of Yacub, the dramatist strives to fix concretely in the minds of the viewers an awareness of the tragic black past. Baraka also supplements the entralling visual effect of this scene with equally affecting sounds and smells—"ship groaning . . . sea smells . . . odors of the sea . . . incense . . . Urine. Excrement . . . African Drums . . . people moaning"—all of which contribute to what he calls a "total atmosfeeling."

The most striking aspect of the text of *Slave Ship* is the generous application of stage directions. Dialogue, the strongest element in Baraka's earliest works, comprises no more than forty per cent of the written text. The remainder of the slim Jihad pamphlet consists of the playwright's copious and vibrantly written instructions, which make for the intensely kinetic quality of the play. The sparse dialogue is generally employed as a more precise or exemplary underscoring of some larger mime-like activity. These pointed interpositions follow the more expansive activity in almost liturgical formality. Perhaps it is this structure that prompts Larry Neal to refer to *Slave Ship* as "ritualized history."[38]

Baraka's method is evidenced early in the play. Following the establishment of the "total atmosfeeling," *i.e.*, the sense of boundless suffering and cruelty, the dramatist intensifies the effect by particularizing the activity. First, we hear the disembodied voices of the white sailors, whose malevolent power is underscored in their vague representation (*"There is just dim light at top of the set, to indicate where voices are...."*).

> VOICE 2: Aye, Aye, Cap'n. We're on our way. Riches be ours, by God.
>
> VOICE 1: Aye riches, riches be ours. We're on our way, America! (*Laughter*)

Against the heedless venality of these voices, Baraka juxtaposes the spirituality of the enslaved blacks, who attempt to hold onto their traditional religions. They moan and implore their gods:

> WOMAN 1: Ooooooooo, Obatala!
>
> WOMAN 2: Shango!
>
> . . . .
>
> MAN 1: Shango, Obatala, make your lightning, beat the inside bright with paths for your people. Beat, Beat Beat [. . .]

This same treatment—general and particularized—is given all the major phases of Afro-American history, as seen by Baraka. Like the creators of the new jazz, Baraka's actors are first urged to present these various phases in a collectively improvised manner. For example, his treatment of the separation of the black family suggests the freed orchestral form of the new music. Baraka captures the spirit of this music in his directions. Note the furious cacophony of this scene: "The moans and pushed-together agony. Children crying incessantly. The mothers trying to calm them. More than one child. Young girls afraid they may be violated. Men trying to break out, or turning into frightened children. Families separated for the first time." Anyone who has heard the music of John Coltrane, Albert Ayler, Sun-Ra, Pharoah Sanders, and read Baraka's generous commentary on that music, needs no further substantiation of the writer's conscious attempt to dramatize the music. Baraka wrote of one performance by Pharoah Sanders: "At the height of the music, the moaning and screaming came on in earnest. This is the ecstasy of the new music. At the point of wild agony or joy, the wild moans, screams, yells of life, in constant change."[39] This is the entire thrust of *Slave Ship*, a "historical pageant".

The generalized scene of separation receives specific treatment in the following exchange:

> WOMAN 2:   Ifanami, Ifanami . . . where you?? Where you?? Ifanami
>   (Cries) Please, oh, God.
> MAN 1:   Obata . . . (Drums beat down, softer . . . humming starts
>   . . . hummmmmmm, hummmmmmmmmm, like old
>   black women humming for three centuries in the slow
>   misery of slavery . . . hummmmmmmmmmmmmmmmmmm-
>   mm, hummmmmmmmmmmmmmmmmmmmmmmmmmm-
>   mm)

This same rendering recurs in the remainder of the history. Following the destruction of the family, the audience witnesses and, of course, participates both in the slaves' Americanization (seen in the taking of English names and the adoption of the Christian faith), as well as their utter degradation, epitomized in the shuffling black slave who betrays Reverend Turner's (presumably Nat's) rebellion. Baraka posits the genesis of the black middle class in this particular slave, who informs on the rebellious preacher for a pork chop. This character is later updated in the modern black preacher, symbol of the Civil Rights Movement, who, Baraka assures us, is "the same tom as before." The drama's only real humor surfaces in the vacuous lines attributed to the spineless preacher:

> Yass, we understand . . . the problem. And, personally, I think some agreement can be reached. We will be non-violent . . . to the last . . . because we understand the dignity of pruty mcbonk and the greasy ghost. Of course diddy rip to bink of vout juice. And penguins would do the same.

Audience involvement is sustained to this point mainly through the physical conditions created by the set. Because most of the activity is still centered in the "hold" of the ship (which is indeed metaphor for the black man's position in America), the attention of the audience remains painfully glued to it. This creates an unavoidable empathy which in no way endears the tom, the preacher, or the ominous white "voices" to the viewer-participants. Although the text, which can hardly substitute for the performed play, does not explicitly indicate other ways of involving the audience, those who have seen the play speak of frequent contact between players and viewer-participants. Dan Isaacs specifically recalls the participatory urge elicited by the intensely personal and direct appeal of the auctioneer. However, after considering the possibly dire consequences of his entering fully into the drama, *i.e.*, buying the slave girl, he opted for the minimal participation of the other viewers. Such improvised overtures abound in the performance of this theatrical analogue to the new music.

Of course, the form itself provokes much of the audience's empathetic response. First, the absence of traditional plot frees the viewer from the completely cerebral, distanced response of conventional theater. The other participatory aspect of the play is seen in the anonymity of the characters. As Stefan Brecht assesses the calculated effect of this factor: "In this play, there are neither heroes nor individuals. Even the embodiments of abstract qualities are not individualized . . . . The acting supports this anonymism, which further distinguishes the kind of play it is. And the play by this aspect makes a statement about the kind of community it upholds. And even about the kind of political action it advocates."[40]

Slave Ship ends with a treatment of the militancy and nationalism of the post-Civil Rights era. The masterful pacing recalls that employed in *Dutchman*. As the rebellious blacks, urged on by a "New-sound saxophone tearing up the darkness," break their shackles and leave the stifling hold of the ship, the viewer-participants simultaneously experience liberty. For they can now fully witness the spectacle without strain. The chant of the former slaves, now making their way up from the hold, echoes the later poems of Baraka. All chant:

> Rise, Rise Rise
> Cut these ties, Black Man Rise
> We gon' be the thing we are . . .
> (Now all sing "When we gonna rise")
> When we gonna rise/up

> When we gonna rise/up
> When we gonna rise
> When we gonna rise up brother
> When we gonna rise above the sun
> When we gonna take our own place,
>   brother
> Like the world has just begun?

The complete communion is saved for the end, after the adversary forces—both the preacher and the voices—have been killed. After this purgative violence, we witness:

> All players fixed in half light, at the movement of the act. Then lights go down. Black. Lights, come up abruptly, and people on stage begin to dance, some hip Boogaloruba, finger pop, skate, monkey, dog . . . Enter audience; get members of audience to dance. To same music music Rise Up. Turns into an actual party. When the party reaches some loose improvisation, *etc.*, audience relaxed, somebody throws the preacher's head into center of floor, *i.e.*, after dancing starts for real. Then black.

The dance serves two vital functions. First, it invites the members of the audience to act out the aggression and violence which they have held in check both during the play and in their everyday lives. In this respect, the "loose improvisation" of this dance provides a real communal exorcism. The dance, with its unifying force, also celebrates the spiritual restoration of the black man. This final scene suggests that the primal energies of the African are now being reasserted, *i.e.*, the former slave has reclaimed those vital elements of his being that were so brutally wrenched from him (recall the frenzied prayers to the lost "Orishas").

Slave Ship stands in relation to the later plays of Baraka in much the same way that *In Our Terribleness* relates to the earlier poetry. Just as the first political poems were characterized by the revolutionary fervor of the early 1960's (recall "Three Movements and a Coda," and "Black People"), the first completely propagandistic plays, best exemplified by *Experimental Death Unit # 1*, communicated this same trend. The poetic attacks on the black bourgeoisie, civil rights leaders, and deluded blacks in general ("Black Bourgeoisie," "Civil Rights Poem," and "W. W.") assume satirical dramatic treatment in *Great Goodness of Life*, and other plays. *A Black Mass,* the dramatic equivalent of the "raising" poems, is distinguished by the same exaggeratedly "spiritual" aura as those poems. In these works the writer seems to equate consciousness-raising with the necessity of restraint or stultification. After straining to reshape the degraded black man into the glorious "ancient image," Baraka seems to conclude suddenly that the image was never completely lost. He asserts that it is present in the tremendous energy of the black style and consequently attempts to infuse his works with this vital energy (compare the incessant movement of *Slave Ship* to the stylized manner of *A Black Mass*). The author perceives a spirituality or African continuity in the vigor of the popular dances of the day, as, for example, in his coingage "boogaloruba," an Africanization of the popular "boogaloo." As he asserts in *In Our Terribleness*, the soulful essence of black life shines brightly just under the veneer of urban depravity. The same message is rendered in even more compelling manner in the electrifying release of *Slave Ship*, Baraka's most ambitious play.

Notes

[1]Larry Neal, "The Black Arts Movement," *The Drama Review*, XII, no. 4 (Summer, 1968): 32.

[2]Theodore Hudson, *From Leroi Jones to Amiri Baraka* (Durham, North Carolina: Duke University Press, 1973), p. 21.

[3]LeRoi Jones, "The Need for a Cultural Base to Civil Rites and Black Power Mooments," in *The Black Power Revolt*, ed: Floyd Barbour (Boston: Porter Sargent Publishers, 1968), p. 125.

[4]Neal, p. 24.

[5]Hudson, p. 24.

[6]*New York Times,* 23 February 1965, p. 40.

[7]Clive Barnes, *New York Times,* 30 November 1971, p. 57.

[8]Saul Gottlieb, "They Think You're an Airplane and You're Really a Bird," *Evergreen Review* (December, 1967): 52.

[9]Hudson, p. 35.

[10]LeRoi Jones, "A Black Value System," *The Black Scholar,* I, no. 4, (November, 1969): 55.

[11]David Llorens, "Ameer (LeRoi Jones) Baraka," *Ebony,* August, 1969, p. 80.

[12]LeRoi Jones, "Philistinian and the Negro Writer," in *Anger and Beyond,* ed: Herbert Hill (New York: Harper & Row, 1968), p. 54.

[13]Jones, Tales, p. 16.

[14]*Ibid.,* p. 16.

[15]Roger D. Abrahams, "Joking: the Training of the Man of Words in Talking Broad," in *Rappin' and Stylin' out,* ed: Thomas Kochman (Urbana: University of Illinois Press, 1972), p. 218.

[16]Stephen Henderson, *Understanding the New Black Poetry* (New York: William Morrow and Company, Inc., 1973), p. 43.

[17]H. Rap Brown, *Die Nigger Die* (New York: Dial Press, 1969), pp. 25-26.

[18]Ellison, p. 486.

[19]Marvin X., "Islam and Black Art: An Interview with Ameer Baraka (LeRoe Jones)," in *Black Arts, an Anthology of Black Creations,* ed: Ahmed Alhamiri and Harun Kofi Wangara (Detroit: Black Arts Press, 1969), p. 151.

[20]Andrew P. Watson, "Negro Primitive Religious Services," in *God Struck Me Dead*, ed: Clifton Johnson (Philadelphia: Pilgrim Press, 1945), p. 5.

[21]Hudson, p. 141.

[22]*Ibid.*, p. 145.

[23]Clyde Taylor, "Baraka as Poet," in *Modern Black Poets*, ed: Donald Gibson (Englewood Cliffs, N. J.: Prentice-Hall, 1973), p. 133.

[24]LeRoi Jones, *Black Music* (New York: William Morrow and Company, 1967), p. 199.

[25]Ishmael Reed, *Mumbo Jumbo* (Garden City, N. Y.: Doubleday & Co., 1972), p. w.

[26]Ed Bullins, "Introduction," *New Plays from the Black Theater* (New York: Bantam Press, 1969), p. viii.

[27]Perry Miller, *The Puritans*, Vol. I, ed: Thomas Johnson (New York: Harper & Row, 1963), p. 65.

[28]Ed Bullins, "A Short Statement on Street Theatre," *The Drama Review*, XII, 4 (Summer, 1968): 93.

[29]LeRoi Jones, "What Does Non-Violence Mean," *Home* (New York: Morrow, 1966), p. 136.

[30]M. D. Anderson, *Drama and Imagery in English Medieval Churches* (Cambridge: Cambridge University Press, 1963), pp. 164-65.

[31]*Ibid.*, p. 2.

[32]Malcolm X and Alex Haley, The Autobiography of Malcolm X (New York: Grove Press, 1965), p. 166.

[33]Imamu Amiri Baraka, "The Fire Must be permitted to Burn Full Up," *Raise Race Rays Raze* (New York: Random House, 1971), p. 119.

[34]*Ibid.*, p. 132.

[35]Roland Reed, "Form and Meaning in Some Plays by Imamu Amiri Baraka," (Ph.D. dissertation, University of Nebraska, 1972), p. 104.

[36]Dan Isaacs, "The Death of the Proscenium Stage," *Antioch Review*, 31:2 (Summer, 1971), p. 250.

[37]*Ibid.*, p. 246.

[38]Neal, p. 37.

[39]LeRoi Jones, *Black Music*, p. 134.

[40]Stefan Brecht, "LeRoi Jones' *Slave Ship*," *The Drama Review*, 14:2 (Winter, 1970); 214.

Chapter IV

Recapitulation

"... there is a sense of the Prodigal about my life that begs to be resolved. But one truth anyone reading these pieces ought to get is the
sense of movement—the struggle, in myself, to understand where and
who I am, and to move with that understanding."[1]

The foregoing affirmation is taken from Baraka's prefatory
remarks to *Home: Social Essays*. In truth, the essays collected therein afford us a precise chart of the author's developing aesthetic and
socio-political consciousness. The early essays from *Home* reflect the
onset of the writer's argument with his old peers, the Village
aesthetes (recall Chapters I and II). In such selections as "Cuba
Libra" and "Letter to Jules Feiffer," he severely castigates the apolitical stance of the aesthetes as well as what he perceives as the in-
effectual theorizing of the so-called "liberal," a favorite whipping
boy of the writer's. The later essays of *Home* show a crystallization
of these attitudes and a nascent black nationalism (see such selections as "Black is a Country," "Street Protest," and "Soul Food").
We witness the full flowering of the nationalist in "The Legacy of
Malcolm X, and the Coming of the Black Nation." Corollary to these
articles are those chronicling the writer's aesthetic reorientation.
Along with the anti-aesthete theme of "Cuba Libra" and other early
essays, Baraka calls for a more thorough investigation of Afro-American life on the part of the black writer (see "The Myth of a 'Negro
Literature' "). This is given further treatment in "A Dark Bag" and
"Black Writing" and carried to its most extreme statement in "The
Revolutionary Theatre" and "State/meant," later works calling for a
thoroughly politicized literature.

Baraka's self-depiction as prodigal voyager to self understanding through struggle is vividly dramatized in his extremely autobiographical fiction. In both *The System of Dante's Hell* and *Tales*, we

see an even more thorough and intensely lyrical recording of the author's psychological "movement." Moreover, both works exemplify the extent of the writer's debt to various major modernists. Of course, the profound influence of Joyce is most prominently present in these works. Like *Ulysses, The System* is a concerted fictional attempt at fully recapturing the life of a specific time and place. Nevertheless the artist uses that life to embody a broad phase of human experience. The Newark of Baraka's youth is recreated with the same particularizing quality of Joyce's Dublin. Also like Joyce, Baraka achieves the desired end of this particularizing through heavy reliance on the stream-of-consciousness technique. However, whereas most of the selections of *Tales* manifest the same generally expressionistic style of *The System*, structurally they are perhaps best understood in terms of such classics of modern American story-telling as *Winesburg* and *In Our Time*. As in these works, the separate stories of *Tales* present the fictionalized life of the author with an organic and cumulative power generally reserved for the "novel."

According to the author, *The System of Dante's Hell* is structured in the manner of *The Inferno*. However, the reader of *The System* realizes immediately that the author's statment must be loosely and liberally interpreted. As in all his borrowings or adaptations from the mainstream culture, Baraka feels totally free to shape ideas and forms to his own usages, thereby claiming them for himself and revitalizing them. An examination of *The System* reveals that Baraka's hell is, indeed, a state of mind. To be precise, it is the mental state of the schizoid poets discussed in Chapter II. Clay and Walker, we recall, suffer intense psychological trauma because of their inability to reconcile the relentless demands of what the poets perceive as a castrating assimilationism on the one hand and authentic black identity on the other. It is this anguish that characterizes Baraka's hell. His "heretic" is the individual who chooses, in the manner of Clay, or the "black puritan," the path of self-denial.

> I put the Heretics in the deepest part of hell, though
> Dante had them spared, on higher ground.
>   It is heresy, against one's own sources, running in
> terror, from one's deepest responses and insights . . . the
> denial of feeling . . . that I see as basest evil.

In sum, this autobiographical "novel" is Baraka's deeply personal examination of the roots of his own "heresy" and that of his closest associates.

The scenario of *The System* is, in large part, a swift, cinematically recollective romp through the Newark of the author's youth. It "communicates," like Baraka's poetry, by the vivid montage of scenes and characters. In the first pages we see images of the despised, spineless, bourgeois neighbors of the narrator:

> Thin brown owners of buicks [. . .] Natives down the street. All dead. All walking slowly towards their lives. Already, each Sunday forever. The man was a minister. His wife was light-skinned with freckles. Their church was tall brown brick and sophisticated. Bach was colored and lived in the church with Handel. Beckett was funeral director with brown folding chairs.

It is the life of these assimilationist "citizens" that the author has persistently rejected. He repeatedly attacks this syndrome through the symbolic use of the church. (Recall *The Baptism* and "Hymn for Lanie Poo.") In the section of *The System* entitled "Hypocrites," the protagonist specifically recalls the class-conscious church of his youth and, in doing so, places us in the midst of the worship. We experience the sight, smells, and sounds of the service:

> The trustees filed in smiling. After they'd brought in the huge baskets of money. They'd smile and be important. Their grandsons would watch from the balcony (if you were middleclass baptists and had some women with pince-nez). Mrs. Peyton was one, but she stank and died skinny in a slum. They'd smile tho. Mr. Blanks, Mr. Russ. A dark man with a beautiful grey mustache.

In the reference to "Mr. Russ," presumably a trustee, we see the author's reminder of the intensely autobiographical nature of this work. (See p. 72) The young protagonist was surely one of the grandsons who "would watch from the balcony." Membership in this particular church was yet another manifestation of the mania for social distinction, for "place," and for a specious orderliness that gave the illusion of a meaningful world.

Place. Place each thing, each dot of life. Each person,
will be PLACED. DISPOSED OF.

Like the protagonist of *The Toilet*, the narrator of *The System* anguishes over his growing allenation from fellow blacks. Using names that appeared in *The Toilet* and in later stories, the author laments his inability to respond to life with the vibrant self-knowledge of his ghetto friends. He envies:

Murray and Ora, hard and living. In light, they still
sprawl in light. A thin bar of shadow on the stone.
they live in light. The prodigal lives in darkness.
[Murray and Ora lived] In the slums.
Even we called them that, but all my
later friends lived there [. . .] They were all hip and
beautiful.

By way of contrast, the narrator enumerates the "advantages" of residing in his own sterile neighborhood:

[. . .] if you could say "South Munn Ave," instead of Dey St. or Hillside Place or Belmont Ave., you had some note. You could watch ofays play tennis. You could come late to scout meetings and be made patrol leader of the flying eagles.

All of these adolescent memories underscore the author's factual statement that he was "the only 'middle-class' chump running with the Hillside Place bads . . . ."[2]

Much of *The System*, especially the earlier parts, is characterized by the tone of Baraka's earliest poems. The "Heathen" sections, both 1 and 2, manifest the general feelings of ennui and despair seen in *Preface to a Twenty Volume Suicide Note*. Herein the narrator departs from the loosely chronological ordering of the novel; instead of the adolescent's reverie, the opening sections convey the dissatisfaction and self-loathing of the adult *litterateur*. These lines could easily have been included in the early collections of verse. He addresses himself:

You've done everything you said you wdn't Everything you said you despised. A fat mind, lying to itself. Unmoving like some lump in front of a window. Wife, child, house, city, clawing at your gentlest parts. Romance become just sad tinny lies. And your head full of them. What do you want anymore? Nothing. Not poetry or that purity of feeling you had.

Along with the imagery of stifling domesticity, the cold urban scene, and alienation (note the frequent use of window imagery), the narrator laments his choice of the reflective life. The poet and editor of the "little magazine" bemoans:

> The simple incompetence of his writing. The white wall smeared with grease from hundreds of heads. All friends. Under his hands like domestic lice. The street hangs in front of the window and does not breathe. Trucks go to New Jersey. The phone rings and it will be somebody he does not even understand. A dope addict who has written short stories.

The narrator's indictment of the reflective life becomes even more explicit in his pointed allusion to the creature Baraka has privately mythologized as Crow Jane. In "Heathen: No. 2," the narrator suggests that he has been undone by this familiar lady:

> The fat breasted fashionable slut of letters. Her blonde companion in the sulking dugouts of stupidity. She clasped my face in her bones and kissed silence into my mouth.

This novel, like most of Baraka's work, beginning with *The Toilet*, is concerned with the writer's overwhelming sense of guilt about his alienation from his "sources." He assures us, however, that he is not alone in this "heresy." Many of his closest associates also succumbed to the blandishments of the dominant culture. In "Hypocrites" he speaks of the smugly successful members of the old gang who fell prey to the "cool scholarship game which turns stone killers alabaster by graduation time."[3] One such success says, from his faceless station:

> Boy, we cool even tho we teach school now and disappeared in our powder-blue coats.

Another group of escapees chides the narrator for his criticism of their various achievements. They gloat:

> Sylvia was part of our scene and you know she was hip. What about Holmes? He's a doctor now, and you know you admired him. He could run and liked to talk about sports. Caesar taught you to hurdle. He had great form. He's a doctor now too. All of us are somewhere. We own trees.

In the section entitled "The Eighth Ditch (Is Drama," Baraka resorts to the same method of dramatizing his split psyche we witnessed in *Dutchman* and *The Slave, i.e.,* the use of antithetical characters. In this particular section of the novel, this theme is treated more explicitly than ever before, however. The two chief characters are numbered "46" and "64." They are obviously the warring factions of the author's psyche, 46, the voice of restraint and middle-class values, 64 the exhuberant voice of excess and the ghetto streets. The whole of Baraka's canon can, in fact, be described in terms of his effort to subject "46" to the will of "64." Recoiling from his black roots, "46" tells "64":

> I delivered papers to some people like you. And got trapped in it; those streets. Their mouths stank of urine, black women with huge brests lay naked in their beds. Filthy mounds of magazines, cakeboxes, children. I cd walk our of yr life as simple as I tossed newspapers down the sewer.

"64 replies:

> I want you to remember me . . . so you can narrate the sorrow of my life. (*Laughs*) My inadequacies . . . and yr own. I want to sit inside yr head and scream obscenities into your speech. I want my life forever wrought up with yours!

The playlet literally climaxes with "64" 's making love to "46." "64" impregnates "46" with the sense of self that he so desperately needs. This section ends with the prospect of "46" 's suffering gang rape by several other street-oriented youths. Once again Baraka puts homosexuality to metaphorical use. However, in contrast to the

earliest portrayals of the homosexual as humanitarian, "The Eighth
Ditch" and later works present the homosexual as the man devoid of
self-knowledge.

Near the novel's conclusion, the experimental manner gives
way to markedly traditional, "story line." In fact, the last two narrative sections, "Circle 9: Bolgia 1—Treachery to Kindred" and "6.
The Heretics" are conventional, self-contained units. Although they
are both essential to the unfolding of the narrator's progress, each
chapter has a unity of its own. Baraka refers specifically to this shift
in narrative mode in the section "Sound and Image," which serves as
an epilogue to the book. He says:

> Hell in this book which moves from sound and image ("association com-
> plexes") into fast narrative is what vision I had of it around 1960-61
> and that fix on my life, and my interpretation of my earlier life.

"Circle 9: Bolgia 1—Treachery to Kindred," subtitled "The
Rape," is the first "fast narrative." Here the narrator explicitly be-
rates himself for his growing alienation from the larger black community. He and his peers, now college students, represent what the
narrator calls "The NEW group," self-imagined future leaders of the
race.

> Summers, during college we were all celebrities. East Orange parties,
> people gave us lifts and sd our names to their friends [. . .] THE
> BEAUTIFUL MIDDLECLASS HAD FORMED AND I WAS TO BE A
> GREAT FIGURE, A GIANT AMONG THEM.

With the onset of bourgeois aspirations, the narrator reevaluates his
priorities, changes his style. Instead of the gritty bistros of Belmont
Avenue (see "The Screamers," *Tales*), the group regularly attended
the more fashionable house parties given by the sons and daughters
of the black middle class. As in earlier works, the author continues to
evince the pervasive influence of E. Franklin Frazier. The boys in
this particular section, all scions of the black middle class, have been
conditioned to think of their education only in terms of its power to
place them forever beyond the bounds of those trapped in the
ghetto. As they take the whore of this narrative beyond the still-

restricted limits of black affluence, the boys dream of the day when
they will have, as proof of their worth, homes in "dark Montclair,"

> With larger whiter homes. Some dirt along the way, which meant to us,
> who knew only cement, some kind of tortured wealth. We would all live
> up here some way.

The contempt the youths hold for their roots is given graphic
symbolic treatment in the episode with the whore. This "drunken
girl, woman, slut" stumbles into fashionable East Orange, scene of
the latest party, bringing the painful reminder of another kind of
black life. On seeing her, the narrator articulates the feeling of his
peers. Collectively they think, "What a desperate sick creature she
was . . ." They also wonder "what she wanted here in their paradise."
Like the grinning black statuette of *Invisible Man* and the old man in
"Kabnis," the concluding section of Jean Toomer's *Cane*, this
woman represents the racial past as well as the still-suffering masses
of black people. Baraka's protagonist, like the protagonists of these
two works, will find no inner peace until he accepts this aspect of
his life. That he is not yet able to do this is seen in his comment
before the attempted rape. The narrator's admission of failure comes
in his description of the irresponsibility of the contemplated act, an
act of treachery to the "blood." (Recall *In Our Terribleness*.) The
boys:

> made to laugh. They made to get into the car. They made not to be
> responsible. All with me. Tho this is new, I tell you now because, some-
> how, it all is right, whatever. For what sin you find me here. It's mine.
> My own irreconcilable life. My blood.

The boys express their utter contempt for the woman and all
she symbolizes in their decision to subject her to gang rape. Indeed
the planned violation, thwarted only by her street wisdom, can be
seen as symbolic murder. Intent on "shoving [their] tender unwash-
ed selves in her eyes and mouth," the boys view this woman in much
the same way that Duff viewed the woman in *Experimental Death
Unit #1*. Through this heinous act, they hope to deny her very humanity, while bolstering their own depraved egos.

There is yet another ironical and skillfully rendered aspect to this episode. The woman is both alluring and repulsive, and the narrator's real pain in this memory is that he wants to love her (not rape her) but cannot. In raping her, he will exhibit acceptance of the rules of middle-class Negro society and his ego. In loving her, he will assert his allegiance to what he perceives to be a more authentic life, that of lower-class blacks and the id. Indeed, he can neither rape nor love her. In this respect sexuality is the vehicle of racial and aesthetic allegory here. Central to the narrator's problem (inability to love or rape) is his spectatorial, self-conscious, artistic self. This episode foreshadows the next, except with crucial differences. In the Bottoms, South, and with Peaches, the narrator is in Id country. He is not much different (except a little older) but the setting and people are, and they overwhelm him and help him break through. Yet the break-through—the ability to "love" Peaches—also has a traumatic aftermath.

"6. The Heretics" is obviously a product of Baraka's Air Force experience. The protagonist is a black northern airman stationed in a small southern town. His fearful attitude toward the South, quite reminiscent of the attitude of Toomer's Kabnis, is evident in the opening paragraph of this section. The pain of the racial past foists itself upon his consciousness:

> Blonde summer in our south. Always it floats down and looks in the broad leaves of those unnamed sinister southern trees. Blonde. Yellow, a narrow sluggish water full of lives. Desires. The crimson heavy blood of a race, concealed in those absolute blacks.

Along with this all-too-painful awareness of his racial being, the protagonist feels the tremendous weight of his assimilationist desires. This burden of double consciousness, the recurring bane of the Barakan protagonist, is rendered even more poignantly in the black G. I.'s reference to the reading that has so irrevocably torn him from all human contact. The self-involved, masturbatory emphasis is most appropriate in the following lines:

> [. . .] I turned away and doubled up like rubble or black figure sliding at the bottom of any ocean. Thomas, Joyce, Eliot, Pound, all gone by

and I thot agony at how beautiful I was. And sat sad many times in latrines fingering my joint.

The protagonist's visit to the black community of the town, "the Bottom", is a journey to the realm of the authentic black self. Both he and his fellow black airmen undertake the trip as alien spirits.

[. . .] We stood [. . .] huge white men who knew the world (our wings) and would give it to whoever showed as beautiful or in sad love smiles, at least willing to love us.

The "two imitation white boys," the two heretics, are unable to blend with the life of the Bottom, the raucous life they heard "Yelling as not to hear the sad breathing world. Turning all music up. Screaming all lyrics." The protagonist and his friend approach this scene with the detachment of slumming bluebloods.

The protagonist's alienation is given more extensive treatment in the relating of his experience with Peaches, the black prostitute. His initial inability to make love to Peaches is symbolic of his inability to face up to his racial identity, indeed, his denial of it. The impotent narrator's failure is given definitive expression in his pitiful comments in the face of Peaches' desire. In words epitomizing his psychic and spiritual distance from Peaches and all that she symbolizes, he whimpers:

'Please you don't know me. Not what's in my head. I'm beautiful. Stephan Dedalus. A mind, here where is only steel. Nothing else. Young pharoah under trees. Young pharoah, romantic, liar. Feel my face, how tender. My eyes. My soul is white, pure white. and soars. Is the God himself.

The protagonist does manage to throw off the weight of double consciousness for a short period with Peaches. After making love to her and sharing a breakfast of watermelon both symbolic of his momentary self-acceptance, the protagonist luxuriates in "the smell of (Peaches), heavy, traditional, secret." He even considers remaining with her, perhaps going permanently AWOL. This fantasy, however, comes to an abrupt end when he, on an errand for Peaches, views a greying sky. The clouds that so often symbolized whiteness and alienation in the earlier poems (see p. *56*) perform the same function here.

> A despair came down. Alien grace. Lost to myself, I'd come back. To that ugliness sat inside me waiting. And the mere sky greying could do it.

The nightmarish narrative ends appropriately with the protagonist in a bitter battle with three black boys, an objective rendering of his continued psychic division. It is even more appropriate that the assimilationist speaker, momentarily crazed by this conflict and hospitalized for it, concludes by noting that he "woke up 2 days later, with white men, screaming for God to help me."

In "Sound and Image," a brief epilogue to *The System of Dante's Hell*, Baraka not only explains the theme of this most difficult of books; he also describes the technique. The novel "moves from sound and image ('association complexes') into fast narrative. . . ." The early sections of the novel are organized around fundamental aspects of the narrator's life, aspects that recur in the manner of musical motifs. Specific names, places, and images give texture and concreteness to the work and manifest the narrator's psychic orientation at each phase of his development. Belmont Avenue and Hillside Place are equated with self-knowledge, while North Newark and East Orange represent self-deceit and self-hatred. The names of certain early friends, Morris, Ora, *et. al.*, referred to as the 'pre-diaspora clan," are likewise juxtaposed with the names of later "lost" peers. Other "association complexes" are seen in the narrator's extremely fluid, yet vivid, recollections of various adolescent fads and preoccupations. In an effort to recapture thoroughly the sensation of his formative years, the narrator moves, with an ultimate self-absorption, from recollections of the fashionable dress of the day (in reference to the narrator's garb, "the green tyrolean with the peacock band. Cool.") to the popular music and dances (referring to one of the more popular of the early rhythm and blues groups of the '50's, "I heard the Orioles sing 'It's too Soon to Know' . . ."), to sand-lot athletics (as a way of remembering old boyhood friends and acquaintances, "Spencer, his name was. Tall & agile & dark. Skinny with long legs, low dangling hands on third base"). All these and other "association complexes" are rendered in a manner suggesting the fitful flux of the mind in process.

The movement toward "fast narrative," or more conventionally plotted sections, is symbolic of the narrator's embryonic grasp of his malaise. These more conventional passages represent a tentative ordering and unifying of the narrator's confused and fragmented life. This ordering is more conclusively effected with the writing of *Tales*.

Tales

Several of the selections in *Tales* were previously published in such journals as *Evergreen Review, Transatlantic Review, Yugen, Pa'lante* as well as the Baraka-edited anthology *The Moderns*. Some of these works were written as early as 1962. Others were composed expressly for the 1967 publication of *Tales*. Despite this discontinuity in its composition, a factor that is also largely responsible for the apparent disjunction of various parts of *The System, Tales* is a remarkably cohesive book. All the major themes we have come to associate with Baraka are present in this collection; moreover, to the informed reader, it is more clearly autobiographical than *The System*. In this treatment of the various sketches and tales, we shall consider the several fictional masks, not in the sequence with which they appear in the collection, but as they relate to the chronology of the artist's life.

We have observed Baraka's power in re-creating the life of the adolescent in *The Toilet*, various poems from *Preface*, such later poems as "Cops," and in various sections of *The System*. We see further evidence of his adept handling of the pre-adolescent in two stories from *Tales*, "Uncle Tom's Cabin: Alternate Ending" and "The Death of Horatio Alger." The protagonists of both stories, sons of the black middle class, are "making a great run for America . . ." As in the earliest works, the author points out the dangers of assimilationism as well as the deceptive nature of the educational process. Both are dominant concerns of all of Baraka's writings. Although "Uncle Tom's Cabin: Alternate Ending" is concerned with both themes, its rather mystifying "tag" suggests a very non-Barakan idealism or racial rapprochement.

A fifth grader in "a grim industrial complex of northeastern America; about 1942," little Eddie McGhee is quite like his creator at this particular stage of the latter's development. Moreover, like Ray of *The Toilet*, Eddie is exceptionally bright. Instead of endearing him to his teacher, as is the case with Ray, however, we see that Eddie's mental prowess disconcerts the rigid and racist Miss Orbach. Nevertheless, the story is about the epiphanic reorientation of Miss Orbach. In the early actions of Miss Orbach, we see the meaning of Baraka's title, "Uncle Tom's Cabin: Alternate Ending." Miss Orbach's attitude is diametrically opposed to that evidenced by Harriet Beecher Stowe in her "Concluding Remarks" (chapter 45) to *Uncle Tom's Cabin*. Speaking of the noble aspirations of the freedman, she says:

> The first desire of the emancipated slave, generally, is for *education*. There is nothing that they are not willing to give or do to have their children instructed; and, so far as the writer has observed herself, or taken the testimony of teachers among them, they are remarkably intelligent and quick to learn. The results of schools, founded for them by benevolent individuals in Cincinnatti, fully establish this.[4]

Miss Orbach clearly does not share Miss Stowe's joy with regard to the black American's intelligence, his enthusiasm for learning, or for that matter, his emancipation. Each of these factors challenges what she perceives as the "natural" ordering of things. Her general conservatism is underscored in the description of her restrained manner and drab dress. The teacher's racial bias is symptomatic of her general antipathy to change and life itself. Baraka explains her unwillingness to confront life by noting that Miss Orbach's burden was:

> The kindly menace of leading a life in whose balance evil was a constant intrigue but grew uglier and more remote as it grew stronger. She would have loved to do something really dirty. But nothing she had ever

heard of was dirty enough. So she contented herself with good, *i.e.*, purity, as a refuge from mediocrity.

Miss Orbach's evasion of life is reflected in her classroom demeanor as well. Faced with her dirty students, she would frequently "drift off into her sanctuary of light and hygiene even though her voice carried the inanities of arithmetic seemingly without delay." The teacher's most painful and constant reminder of her personal malaise comes in the form of little Eddie McGhee, the affable and precocious black student.

Quite different from the typical alienated Baraka hero, Eddie is the kind of child who would be considered, under today's all-too-frequent diagnosis, "hyperactive." His openness is reflected in the tactile nature of his relationship to his classmates. Eddie kisses and touches his classmates and is kissed and touched in return. (Speaking of Miss Orbach, the narrator says, "how the social doth pain the anchorite.") The cloistered teacher sees a personal affront in Eddie and his all-encompassing, life-affirming eyes. Hence her guilt-ridden attempt to have him diagnosed as abnormal. Miss Orbach is in dire need of spiritual rejuvenation, and the narrator intimates that this rejuvenation comes as a result of her confrontation with Eddie's mother, Louise McGhee.

Like Ray's mother, alluded to in *The Toilet*, Louise McGhee is a middle-class black mother militantly bent on the refinement of her son. Indeed, she is proof of Miss Stowe's assertion that, "There is nothing that they are not willing to give or do to have their children instructed. . . ." On the one hand, Louise McGhee's forceful self-assertion, born of love, is an affront to Miss Orbach's spiritual torpor. On the other, however, it is a challenge. Hence the conclusion:

> When Miss Orbach got to the principal's office and pushed open the door she looked directly into Louise McGhee's large brown eyes, and fell deeply and hopelessly in love.

This story offers an "alternate" ending to *Uncle Tom's Cabin* because it is the black who does the teaching in this case. Because black can teach white to love, the story also hints that love *can* exist between black and white, thus undercutting the author's more pessimistic statements. Although the typically Barakan digressive and didactic passages attempt to assert racial antagonism as the overwhelming issue, it is never quite effected. This particular theme is given more convincing treatment in "The Death of Horatio Alger," the story which follows "Uncle Tom's Cabin: Alternate Ending."

Mickey, the adult narrator of "The Death of Horatio Alger," recalls an incident which occurred when he was approximately the same age as little Eddie McGhee. His is the burden of self-hatred and self-denial. In the "digressive" passage of the story, he recalls his high school days as sports editor of a high school paper "which should have been printed in Italian. . . ." It was during his high school years that he became aware of his assimilationist desires. As usual this relationship with the dominant culture is seen in terms of his attachment to a white woman. It was at this point that the narrator became enamored of :

> Light freckles, sandy hair, narrow clean bodies. Though none live where I lived then [. . .] I saw [. . .] young American girls, for the first time. And have loved them as flesh things emanating from real life, that is, in contrast to my own, a scraping and floating through the last three red and blue stripes of the flag, that settles the harsh of the lower middle class.

Mickey is completely dedicated to the attainment of this "other" life and all of his actions attest to the degree of his contempt for what the narrator of *The System* calls his "sources." In looking back on his pre-adolescent days, Mickey realizes just how dominant the "alien" worldview of the dominant culture was in shaping not only his thoughts and actions but those of his peers as well. This is brought out in the spare story of his altercation with J. D.

The narration of the encounter itself is a crystallization, an objective epitome, of the negative influence of the dominant culture on the behavior of black Americans. Through this highly symbolic altercation, Baraka asserts that white society exerts a sinister and distorting pressure on the deep-rooted and natural inclinations of blacks. Although J. D. knows full well the harmless, almost ritualistic nature of the "dozens" when played among real friends, he allows the misapprehensions of his white peers to dictate his violent response to Mickey:

> And J., usually a confederate, and private strong arm, broke bad be-
> cause Augie, Norman, and white Johnny were there, and laughed, mis-
> understanding simple 'dozens' with ugly insult, in that curious scholar-
> ship the white man affects when he suspects a stronger link than sociol-
> ogy, or the tired cultural lies of Harcourt, Brace sixth-grade histories.
> And under their naivete he grabbed my shirt and pushed me in the snow.

Much like the "battle royal" in Ellison's *Invisible Man*, the
fight between these two black boys is carried out to the full satisfac-
tion of on-looking whites. To be sure, Baraka is also suggesting that
the dominant culture has long thrived on this intra-group violence,
born of ignorance of self. Yet he suggests simultaneously that beneath this behavior there is the shackled libido desperately seeking
release. As in *The Toilet*, violence is the substitute for love. The narrator lets us know this in no uncertain terms. Describing his final
verbal assault on J. D., he says:

> I called to him for help really. But the words rang full of dead venom.
> I screamed his mother a purple nigger with alligator titties. His father a
> bilious white man with sores on his jowls. I was screaming for help in
> my hatred and loss, and only the hatred would show.

The extreme complexity of Mickey's plight is symbolic of the general
condition of the black American, bound by a love-hate relationship
with himself and his fellow blacks. This idea is given an additional
poignancy in the story's concluding family "portrait," wherein the
relationship between the misunderstanding father and the suffering
son reflects that of the larger racial family.

As stated earlier, Baraka's sketches of adolescence are among
his most impressive creations. This is particularly true of the narratives of the thought-ravaged teen-agers of *Tales*. In such works as
"The Screamers" and "Alighieri's Dream," we literally follow the ad-
ventures of the narrator of *The System*. The sketches are characterized by the same essential concerns that so pervade the longer work.
In both cases we find a narrator, painfully aware of his alienated
status, who wants above all to merge with his "sources" and to flee
all that hinders that merger. "The Screamers," originally published in

The Moderns and a shining example of Baraka's narrative ability, could be justifiably called *The System* in microcosm.

In terms of the author's technique, "The Screamers" is identical to the stories considered earlier. Like "Uncle Tom's Cabin: Alternate Ending" and "The Death of Horatio Alger," it begins with an extremely personal and particular experience, moves to "digressive" general statements concerning the forces that shaped the author/persona, and concludes with the climactic and didactic depiction of the original particularized incident. The action proper of "The Screamers" takes place in a lower-class black night spot in Newark during the early 1950's. As is the case in the majority of Baraka's stories, however, this is literally only half the story. The other half is derived from those stream-of-consciousness "digressions" that do nothing to advance the spare "story line" itself, but which nevertheless contribute immeasurably to the author's overall meaning.

One reviewer aptly called the works collected in *Tales* "lyric poem-stories." To be sure, the narratives frequently remind the reader of Baraka's verse efforts. Note the narrator's introduction to "The Screamers":

> Lynn Hope adjusts his turban under the swishing red green yellow shadow lights. Dots. Suede heaven raining, windows yawning cool summer air, and his musicians watch him grinning, quietly, or high with wine blotches on four-dollar shirts.

This passage is, of course, marked by the Williams-derived concreteness that characterized so much of the writer's early poetry. There is also evidence of his suggestive power in the lyrical description of the steaming, smoky atmosphere of the club. In such stories as "The Screamers," the writer frequently expresses the intense emotionalism of black urban life in the only language equal to the task, *i.e.*, the language of poetry—language that functions essentially through sight and sound rather than denotation.

The unnamed hero of "The Screamers" is one of Baraka's strongest fictional projections of himself. Like the central figures in already discussed works, this young man carries the burden of his separation most heavily. Hungrily exploring the dives of black Newark, the adolescent hero seeks the authentic life denied him by his upwardly moble, assimilationist parents. He experiences this vital and earthy mode only during his clandestine visits to downtown Newark. In the Nitecap, The Hi-Spot, Lloyd's and Graham's he finds:

> A greasy hipness, down-ness, nobody in our camp believed (having social-worker mothers and postman fathers [. . .]

"Our camp" is, of course, that sector of black life fiercely bent on eradicating all vestiges of the racial past. The narrator speaks ferociously of their sterile lives:

> They plotted in their projects for mediocrity, and the neighborhood smelled of their despair. And only the wild or very poor thrived in Graham's or could be roused by Lynn's histories and rhythms. America had choked the rest, who could sit still for hours under popular songs, or be readied for citzenship by slightly bohemian social workers. They rivaled pure emotion with wind-up record players that pumped Jo Stafford into Home Economics rooms.

As in other instances, Baraka guages self-knowledge and black authenticity according to musical taste and response. Those blacks who remain close to their "sources" manifest this in their passion for sounds steeped in the Afro-American musical experience. Evidence of the writer's high regard for the social meaning of this music is seen in his reference to Lynn's "histories." This phrasing reminds us of the study *Blues People* (written at about the same time as the story), Baraka's detailed documentation of Afro-American musical expression as the most precise "chronicler" of the black American's existence. The music, according to Baraka, is always an expression of the racial consciousness of the day. Hence Lynn and his musicians are called "Ethnic historians, actors, priests of the unconscious." The top hornmen of the day are treated in much the same way that beatnik writers had celebrated them earlier. Baraka's deification of such exemplary figures as Illinois Jacquet, Gatortail Jackson, and Gene Ammons ("Jug") recalls Jack Kerouac's ecstatic praise of similar figures in *On the Road*. For both writers the jazz musician symbolizes authenticity and life unfetterd by the dehumanizing forces of convention. His creations are tonal onslaughts against all that would shackle the human spirit. Baraka's screaming tenormen, as well as those of Kerouac, are involved in a "completely nihilistic act."

As the ruminative narrator focuses again on the "story" of the particular night in question, we are better able to understand Lynn Hope's meaning. Hope, whose name signals the indomitable aspiration of his hearers, is the priest who involves his fans in a communal act of affirmation. He leads them in a symbolic destruction of their stifling environs. The ritualistic aspect is underscored in the following remarks by the narrator, who says:

> I had a little cup full of wine a murderer friend of mine made me drink, so I drank it and tossed the cup in the air, then fell in line behind the last wild horn man, strutting like the rest of them

In the narrator's action we see his rejection of parental and societal influence. Completely involved in the sacramental festivity, he recognizes the revolutionary implications of the fervent outpouring of natural energies. The communal nature of the festivity is also emphasized in the scream itself (*i.e.*, the repated "uhh, yeh"), which strongly suggests two bodies in sexual rhythm. This interpretation is strengthened in light of the narrator's humorous remark just prior to the climactic street confrontation. Speaking of the desire of the part of the dancers for even more provocative music, he says, "We had not completely come." The scream symbolizes human fulfillment. Unfortunately, however, the dominant culture is incapable of seeing such meaning in this spontaneous release. Hence the tragically ironic conclusion, born of the misinterpretation of the communal, self-affirming black action. This conclusion makes "The Screamers" one of the most vivid expressions of Baraka's conviction that the black American inhabits an alien world, a world that does not understand his motives and desires.

"A Chase (Alighieri's Dream)," the first selection in *Tales*, is another examination of the adolescent experiences of Baraka's representative hero. In title as well as manner of presentation this work recalls *The System*. The eliptical style has been astutely described by Larry G. Coleman:

> The first story, "A Chase (Aligheri's Dream)," in a series of short flashing telegraphic images, imposes a dreamlike atmosphere over the Newark ghetto where Jones grew up. The extreme sensitivity of the young persona dreamer emerges from beneath a frenetic rapid cataloguing of scenes and people in these New Jersey streets. The narrative itself moves

like the rapid shifts in the musical phrasing of an intricate piece of improvisation.[5]

Out of this impressionistic verbal collage, we are able to feel again the presence of the protagonist of "The Screamers." As he passes various persons and landmarks, we see evidence of the familiar fears and doubts. Holding only contempt for the bourgeois life, he shuns their neighborhoods, for:

> They pace in wool jails, wool chains, years below the earth. Dead cocks crawling, eyes turned up in space.

"Respectably" garbed, *i.e.*, in contrast to the "loud" fashions worn by denizens of the ghetto, these persons recall the walking dead, the "shades" of *The System*.

This sketch is marked by a terrific sense of flight, the flight of a young man who knows, perhaps, that he is in violation of parental dicatates. This motif assumes additional impetus through the use of football imagery near the end of the sketch. In this passage, the narrator imagines himself eluding all pursuers in a dramatic scoring run. The best evidence of the speaker's plight is seen in the story's conclusion, however. Here we are given the distinct impression that he is frantically returning to the world of respectability, after a night of visitation in that world more thoroughly examined in "The Screamers" and the final section of *The System*. The speaker, on returning, even clothes himself in the detested garb of the "dead":

> A long stretch from Waverly to Spruce (going the other way near Hillside). A long stretch, and steeper, straight up Spruce. And that street moved downtown. They all passed by, going down. And I was burning by, up the hill, toward the Foxes and the milk bar. Change clothes on the street to a black suit. Black wool. 4 corners, the entire world visible from there. Even to the lower regions.

Ray, the protagonist of "The Alternative," is, like Clay of *Dutchman*, a student at a black college. In this realistic recreation of dormitory life, we can be sure that Baraka draws heavily on his experience as a student at Howard University and that this story is primarily an indictment of what he perceived as the black college's failures. The same indictment is repeated in such works as "Poem for Half White College Students," and *The Death of Malcolm X*, a later play. In these works he excoriates the black college for turning out black automatons whose vision is myopically set on material gain and a place among the deluded black middle class. Like Ralph Ellison and E. Franklin Frazier before him, Baraka also indicts the college for suppressing the black student's authentic sense of self. Frazier says:

> The only concession that was made to the Negro's culture was that the students were required to sing Spirituals for the white visitors. But though the school was saturated with religious feeling, the required religious activities were designed to wean them from the religious emotionalism of the Negro.[6]

In statements concerning the fictional black college of *Invisible Man*, Ellison renders the same judgment. In the following passage his hero, on the verge of expulsion, reflects on the effectiveness of the black college as the cause of cultural shame:

> And here, sitting rigid, I remember the evenings spent before the sweeping platform in awe and in pleasure, and in the pleasure of awe; remember the short formal sermons intoned with calm assurances purged of that wild emotion of the crude preachers most of us knew in our home towns and of whom we were deeply ashamed, these logical appeals which reached us more like the thrust of a firm and formal design requiring nothing more than the lucidity of uncluttered periods, the lulling movement of multi-syllabic words to thrill and console us. And I remember, too, the talks of visiting speakers, all eager to inform us of how fortunate we were to be a part of the 'vast' and formal ritual. How fortunate to belong to this family sheltered from those lost in ignorance and darkness.[7]

It is in this perspective that we must view the college and students of "The Alternative." This thinly-fictionalized institution would also separate the man from his "sources."

In the story, Mr. Bush, the dormitory director, personifies the school's assimilationist orientation. As he approaches Ray's boisterous room, Ray imagines the thoughts going through Mr. Bush's mind and scathingly describes his manner simultaneously:

> He could narrow his eyes even in that affluence. Put his hands on his hips. Shove that stomach at you as proof he was an authority of the social grace . . . a western man, no matter the color of his skin. How to? He was saying, this is not the way. Don't act like that word. Don't fail us. We've waited for all you handsome boys too long. Erect a new world of lies and stocking caps. Silence and a reluctance of memory. Forget the slow grasses, and flame, flame in the valley. Feet bound, dumb eyes begging for darkness. The bodies moved with the secret movement of the air. Swinging.

This passage is marked by Baraka's skillful invocation of ethnic humor. No black American of speaking age would miss the humor of, "Don't act like that word." When black elders want the best behavior from their youngsters, they frequently intone, in the manner of Mr. Bush, "Don't act like a Nigger." Nor would many blacks miss the humor of "Erect a world of lies and stocking caps." Many were the black boys and men who, in ritual manner, donned stocking caps on Saturday nights in hopes of whiter Sunday heads. The humor of this passage is swiftly undercut, however, by the suggestive imagery of a lynching. It is this truth of black suffering, Baraka suggests, that the Mr. Bushes of the world, and the colleges they represent, would forget.

The extremely sensitive narrator of "The Alternative," Ray, the "leader," carries the double consciousness of Clay. He, too, is torn between the desire for black identity and the pull of assimilationism. The latter is objectified in his literary interests, while the former is seen in his guilt-ridden relationship with his peers. Like Ray of *The Toilet*, Ray, the college student, wants to be looked upon as "one of the boys." Ironically enough, however, he is accepted primarily because of his assimilationist tendencies. Ray's peers, all of whom are furiously bent on escaping their black roots, look upon Ray as a model. Because he reads constantly and speaks "proper," the other students, the embryonic black middle class, feel that Ray has found that vital key to the other world, the world of the dominant culture. Hence, he is the "leader." However, the schizophrenia of the leader, as well as that of his fellow black collegians, is rendered most objectively in the scene immediately following Mr. Bush's intrusion. As the other boys play cards and Ray reads, the starkness of their psychic division is presented in symbolic language:

> [. . .] he sits reading in green glasses. As, 'No, no, the utmost share/ Of my desire shall be/Only to kiss that air/ That lately kissed thee.' 'Uhh! What's trumps, dammit!'
>
> As tell me not, Sweet, I am unkind,/ That from nunnery/ Of thy chaste breast and quiet mind/ To war and arms I fly.' 'You talking about a light weight mammy-tapper, boy, you really king.' [. . .] As, 'Hardly are those words out when a vast image out of *Spiritus Mundi*/ Troubles my sight: somewhere in sands of the desert/ A shape [. . .] 'Damn, Charlie, we brought back a frank for everybody . . . now you want two. Wrong sunafabitch!'

In this stark juxtaposition of idioms, we see the options available to Ray. This story, like most of Baraka's work, is again evidence of the author's sorrow at having chosen the seemingly nobler path represented by the euphonious lines of Lovelace and Yeats.

In "The Alternative" we see also a return to the pervasive homosexual theme articulated in *The Baptism, The Toilet, The Slave,* and *The System.* This particular invocation of the theme seems to parallel the author's latter employment of it, *i.e.,* as in *The System.* Ray's attraction toward the homosexuals of the story is intended to reflect the degree to which he has been divested of self-knowledge by his "artsy" and literary pursuits. The homosexual has taken on a symbolic value relevant to the racial theme. He epitomizes the black bourgeois malaise. Note the comments of the homosexual postal worker of "The Alternative." In his remarks we see both his self-hatred and his false sense of security, a la Court Royal (see p. *145*).

> Oh, Bobby, you ought to stop being so conscious of being coloured. It really is not fashionable. [. . .] I've got one of those gooood jobs, honey. U. S. guvment [. . .] The P. O. with the rest of the fellas. But it's enough for what I want to do.

The actions of Rick and the other boys, in spite of their ostensible abhorrence of the homosexuals, must really be seen in terms of their latent homosexuality. As with the boys of *The Toilet*, they disguise their deeper desires through acts of aggression. They are in fact, attracted to homosexuality and all that it symbolizes. This is underscored in the author's contempt for them. As he sees them at the height of their perverse jubilations, the narrator observes:

> Doctor, judges, first negro director of welfare chain, mortician, chemists, ad men, fighters for civil rights, all admirable, useful men.

In prophesying the future vocations of his peers, Ray sees them as opportunistic leeches, preying on the very people they attempt to repudiate. As products of the black college, they will surely attempt to further the separation from their sources, but they will not be averse to capitalizing on black suffering.

At least two selections from *Tales* chronicle Baraka's emergence as "writer." Filtered through the consciousness of the poet of *The Dead Lecturer*, these stories exhibit an anti-intellectualism tantamount to that seen in those earlier poems. Like the poet, the narrator of "Salute" comes to doubt the worth of the reflective life. After informing the reader of his first real attachment to the world of books, the narrator debases the merit of his literary pursuits with the following remarks:

> [. . .] the only real thing reading does for anyone is to shut them up for a few hours, and let the other senses function as usefully as the mouth. Quiet already, a young man will grow sullen. Sullen, he will grow into stone. But any 'normal' most times noisy city half-slick young college type hipster will close his mouth for all times, so ugly will have been his re-evaluation of the world, and his life.

As in the earlier works, the artist in search of commitment castigates himself for succumbing to the lure of the literary life, which is presented more and more as an emasculating force. When we realize in this story that it is the nascent artist's love of *belles lettres* which makes possible his accommodation to the dehumanization of Air Force life, we understand more clearly the intensity of this indictment. Perhaps the ultimate statement on the "evils" of the reflective life is seen in "Heroes Are Gang Leaders."

The narrator of "Heroes Are Gang Leaders" is a hospitalized writer, surrounded by the dregs of New York City. Although we are never informed of the writer's particular physical ailment, we are immediately apprised of his spiritual illness. The story begins, "My concerns are not centered on people." From our examination of the earlier works, we know that the increasingly political Baraka takes this statement to be representative of far too many artists. The narrator, furthermore, exhibits the earlier poets disgust for his entrapment in the closed circle of the aesthetes. He says:

> I hope [. . .] That I am not merely writing poems for Joel Oppenheimer or Paul Blackburn . . . but everything alive. Which is not true. Which is simply not true.

The ultimate indictment of the disengaged writer is rendered, however, in this story's central irony. As the Hemingwayesque inquisitors of the helpless Kowalski become more persistent, the narrator attempts desperately to lose himself in his reading, thereby evading his duty to perform an important act of courage. The tragedy of the tale lies in the narrator's willingness to cooly study fictional heroism rather than assert the real thing in the real world. He ends the story with this statement concerning the ugly tableau at his bedside:

> It is the measure of my dwindling life that I returned to the book to rub out their image, and studied very closely another doomed man's life.

In Lew Crosby, the protagonist of the quite conventionally narrated "Going Down Slow," we see another man doomed by his overly reflective pursuits. Crosby must surely be interpreted as a fictional projection of Baraka, the Village-dwelling artist. Of course, his story is told like most of the stories, from the vantage point of the socio-politically committed writer. Lew Crosby is the artist whose vacuum-packed literary preoccupations have divorced him totally from human community. Torn between the demands of domesticity and art, he chooses art—with no attempt at compromise. Even after he learns that this attitude has driven his wife to adultery, he asks himself:

> How can you read *Pierre* if you think your wife's doing something

weird? Then you got to take time out to think about *her*. Oh boy . . .
and then what? How much time can you waste like that? A poem [. . .]
I am Lew Crosby, a writer. I want to write what I'm about, which is
profound shit. Don't ask me anything. Just sit there if you want to
[. . .] Don't try to involve your self with me.

The bane of self-involvement, so often scorned in *The Dead Lecturer*, invites additional censure throughout this story. It opens with
Crosby "in conversation with himself," and "knowing that he was a
comfort to himself." Crosby's egocentricity is given emphatic treatment also at the story's conclusion. After Crosby takes the heroin,
the narrator says, "He sat so far away from anything you can name."
In his final embryonic pose, perhaps symbolic of his immature social
consciousness, Crosby is, moreover, said to be "just out of everybody's reach." There is, indeed, every indication that he is about to
join his victim, Mauro (undoubtedly symbolic of the writer's murder-
ed artistic self). Like the singer of the traditional blues song from
which the story receives its title, Lew crosby foresees his death:

> I have had my fun if I don't get well no mo'
> I have had my fun if I don't get well no mo'
> My health is failin' me, and I'm goin' down slow.

"Words" is evidence of the writer's attempting to find community with those "ignorant motherfuckers who have never read a
book in their lives" (Recall *The Slave*).

> When I walk in the streets, the streets don't yet claim me, and people
> look at me knowing the strangeness of my manner, and the objective
> stance from which I attempt to 'love' them.

Again, Larry Coleman is quite right in stating that this particular selection is "clearly about the artist's alienation from his kinsman
while it explores, for the first time in *Tales*, a way of eliminating that
alienation."[8] The artist, like those around him, sees emptiness in his
previous pursuits. He meets criticism in all quarters:

> Last night in a bar a plump black girl sd, 'O.K., be intellectual, go write
> some more of them jivey books [. . .] she sd 'Why're you so cold
> [. . .]'

In this sketch the themes of identity and commitment coalesce. The artist wants not only to reestablish his ties to his people. He also wants to contribute concretely to their struggle for human dignity. This he feels he cannot do with "them jivey books" or mere "words." The indictment of words is another expression of the attitude seen earlier in the "Crow Jane" poems (see pages 54-57). As in those previous works, the writer flagellates himself for luxuriating in the quarter of the aesthetes, thereby evading the demands of the real world. He laments the time spent "In the closed circle I have fashioned." In the final rejection of the old way, the writer attacks what he now perceives as the evasiveness and general vapidity of his early creations. They are no more than:

> invisible sound vibrations, humming in emptiness, and ideas less than humming, humming, images collide in empty ness, and we build our emotions into blank invisible structures which never exist, and are illusion and pain and madness. Dead whiteness.

"Words" ends with a poem recalling those treated in the third chapter of this study. Like those works, this one is marked by extreme syntactic and thematic simplicity. Immediately following the last indictment of his old forms, this poem is a harbinger of the works to come. This aspect is given additional emphasis in that the work is dated "Harlem 1965." Moreover, the end of alienation is intimated in the pronounced employement of the pronoun "we," in marked contrast to the "I's," "myself's," and "me's" of the early lines. Resolved to dedicate his life and art to changing the conditions under which the masses of black people live, the narrator concludes:

> We turn white when we are afraid
> We are going to try to be happy.
> We do not need to be fucked with.
> We can be quiet and think and love the silence.
> We need to look at trees more closely
> We need to listen.

The sketch "New-Sense" is even more forceful than "Words" in its repudiation of the past. Along with the familiar rejection of what he has come to call "diseased intellectualism," the narrator of this essentially autobiographical piece chides himself for past involvement with white lovers. His statements here bear out my earlier comment on the symbolic indentification of such figures as Lula (*Dutchman*) and "Crow Jane." Possession of and acceptance by these personages meant human fulfillment for the character in flight from self. In this sketch, however, the narrator combines treatment of his literal involvement with the white woman with those values so often represented by Baraka's figurative females. In this most straightforward statement of the problem that has menaced him from *Preface to Tales*, the committed artist champions action and its exponents, *i.e.*:

> the straight ahead people, who think when that's what's called for, who don't when they don't have to. Not the Hamlet burden, which is white bullshit, to always be weighing and measuring and analyzing, and reflecting. The reflective vs. the expressive. Mahler vs. Martha and The Vandellas. It's not even an interesting battle.

Along with an increasing celebration of the exuberance of the black musical style, the latter sketches and tales are also notable for their frequent allusions to literature produced by black Americans. In discussing the relative merits of the "reflective" and "expressive" modes, for example, Baraka refers specifically to the characters Jake and Ray of Claude McKay's novel *Home to Harlem*. The writer who alluded so frequently to Melville, Joyce, Ford Madox Ford, Eliot, and others, has undergone a dramatic reorientation.

Other late selections from *Tales* evidence the writer's post-"Words" psyche. The narrator of "Unfinished," for example, is the studious observer of black urban life. To be sure, he watches from the infamous vantage point of those slick articulators of black despair, the comfortable future leaders and spokesmen designated in "The Alternative." The narrator, now a "celebrated" race spokesman—much like the lionized author of *Dutchman*—is extremely critical of the self that once basked in the glow of that fame.

Like the other patrons of Jocks, the narrator is an assimilationist "dancer," *i.e.*, one who skillfully steps around the reality of black existence. Jocks, mentioned in the poem "Black Art" as the "in" spot for the black bourgeoisie, is a veritable fantasy land. Therein we see those people described so fully by Frazier, those thoroughly intoxicated by:

> The gaiety of pretension. These creeps won't even get like in the Harlem
> Club, and tear the windows out. These cool Knee Crows who have a
> few pesos in their pockets (earned by letting whitey pass gas in their
> noses). There is a cruel frustration drifts through places like that . . .
> places filled with young and old black boushies . . . And you could think
> about white invisible things being dragged back and forth across the ceil-
> ing. Maybe they are talismans of white magic, secret, hideous, ofay
> mojos, their god waves back and forth over black people's heads, making
> them long to be white men. It's too horrible to think about shit like that.

The guilt-ridden narrator wants desperately to deny any kinship to
the "boushies" who frequent Jocks. He knows, however, that beneath his facade of social consciousness there lies an egotism and pretension tantamount to that of any of the detested "dancers." Hence
the narrator's shaky disavowal, "But it wasn't me anyway. I'm here
writing, this never happened to this person. It was somebody else."
In this elusive and cryptic "tale," the narrator splits himself very literally into two personalities. On the one hand, there is "L," former
"dancer" and fashionable black leader/spokesman. On the other,
there is a new man who is struggling with the evil of egocentricity.

The sudden appearance of the cripple, who is reality forcing
his way into Jocks, causes the writer to reevaluate himself and to
question his former motives. He makes him examine his assimilationist tendences:

> I heard your thing,
> can you dig mine. You
> a success in the West,
> aint that a mess. Up in
> Your ches' Polluted
> Stream. Dead fish,
> animals still to evolve.
> A fluke, like black and
> white together in the
> same head or bed, it
> makes no never mind.

There is also the writer's familiar guilt at having chosen the path of letters. Again, this is rendered in terms of perversion. Like several of Baraka's alienated protagonists, this one's assimilationist tendency is projected through the employment of the homosexual theme:

'Arrest Him For Sodomy . . . He Fucked Melville.'

The cripple represents a more authentic black life in that he has endured, despite his having suffered intensely. His perpetual smile, which intimidates the egocentric narrator, is evidence of his attitude toward life. He jolts the old self of the narrator, *i.e.*, "the philosopher of need" (recall the poem "Balboa, the Entertainer"), into an awareness of his shortcomings. A casualty of the system, the cripple represents an experience and vision not accessible to the old writer, a product of academia. Hence, the cripple's concluding song, which seems to transform even Jocks and the plastic people therein. Like the apparent dregs of *In Our Terribleness*, this victim, in actuality, manifests a profound spirituality, and his song is an offering of love.

"Unfinished," like several other selections from *Tales*, is indicative of both Baraka's strengths and weaknesses as a writer of fiction. The spontaneity of this particular "story" forces the reader to delve into the innermost recesses of his imagination. In order to come to terms with these thoughts-put-down-on-the-run, the reader must be as much creator as the writer. "Unfinished" is, indeed, "unfinished," if we think of it in terms of the traditional story. The writer seems to strive for the effect of incompleteness in this and other examples of mind in motion. Not infrequently even Baraka concedes that the stories are incomprehensible. Note the concluding line to New Spirit": "And I know this doesn't make sense." In this same light, recall the cryptic statement in "The Screamers." The young narrator, in search of a dance partner, asks "Who would I get? (Not anyone who would understand this)." All too often the writer does push his tantalizing suggestiveness to the point of diminishing returns. In such instances, "story" becomes mere "puzzle," very nearly losing all claim to artistic meaning. The problems are compounded in "Unfinished" by the author's seemingly deliberate ambiguity with regard to point-of-view and his extreme privacy of allusion. Such purely experimental works merit little critical regard and are of interest only to the reader with a consuming fascination with the writer himself. These same problems cloud such latter selections as "No Body No Place" and "Now and Then," both of which express dissatisfaction with certain nationalistic elements. The author's protracted search for peace within the confines of a healthy black community comes to an end in the darkly humorous "Answers in Progress."

In this final story, called "Black Power science fiction"[9] by one reviewer, we see the author's projected image of the crumbling inner cities of the United States—an extrapolation of the situation in *The Slave*. The setting of this particular story is post-revolution Newark, and the black revolutionaries are busily establishing the new order. In doing so, they summarily execute all representatives of the old system. The remnants of the old dominant culture will survive only if they accept the new order and its values. Corruption in government and the capitalist ethic are things of the past. Moreover, there is the distinct implication that the new world life style is one characterized by the pulse of the Afro-American. Even the blue spacemen, who appear to have been simply biding their time until their earthling brothers got themselves together, attest to the universal hegemony of the new order. Having kept up with the affairs of earth, the spacemen are so "hip" that their first desire is to know where Art Blakey and the Jazz Messengers are playing. The spacemen are, moreover, so nationalistically oriented that they reject the records of the integrated edition of the Messengers. This is evidenced in their scorn for "Buttercorn Lady," a Blakey album which featured white sidemen for the first time. The spacemen acknowledge their blackness not only through their all-consuming interest in jazz (they are adept at scat singing). They even walk black. The narrator says:

> I swear one of those cats had a hip walk. Even though they was hoppin and bopadoppin up and down like they had to pee. Still this one cat had a stiff tentacle when he walked.

Recall the constant reference in earlier poems to the hip walk as significant expression of ethnicity.

In this "utopian" vision, love is "heavy in the atmosphere." Inspirational songs, which, "incidentally," sound very much like the healing poems discussed in Chapter III, are piped throughout the city. The narrator quotes appropriate lines from Claude McKay and likens his emotional state to that of Charlie Parker when Parker dared to explore new musical vistas. The allusions, musical and literary, are noticeably black throughout this story.

In this fictional community, we see a projection of priest-poet-politician Baraka's "New Ark"-based organization, which he envisioned as an exemplary nucleus dedicated to organizing and healing the city's broken black majority. The virtues of brotherly love, discipline, and a strong family unit, all too frequently missing in the black community, are noticeably present in this particular tale. Also remark the importance placed on community art projects in this society. Like the activities carried on at Spirit House, agit-prop theatre is an integral part of "nation'building" in this story. The revolutionary community not only has its cultural arm, however. It reflects, if only by implication, the complete "Black Value System" espoused by Baraka and Ron Karenga (see *The Black Scholar*, November, 1969: The Seven Principles are *Umoja* [Unity], *Kujichagulia* [Self-Determination]. *Ujima* [Collective Work and Responsibility], *Ujamaa* [Cooperative Economics], *Nia*, [Purpose], *Kuumba* [Creativity], *Imani* [Faith].)

Although this final selection is offered as metaphorical proof of the author's replacement of the old ogres of assimilation, bourgeois pretension, and art-for-art's sake with the virtues of black identity and total revolutionary commitment, the story nevertheless communicates a gnawing uncertainty. This uncertainty is, perhaps, most glaringly reflected in the story's essentially comic vision. The only completely comic selection in the book, "Answers in Progress" almost seems to be an afterthought. Following the troubled questing music of the earlier narratives, the melody of the last sounds like the piping of the proverbial whistler in the dark.

In spite of the many works and years separating them, the author of "Answers in Progress" merely creates his own comic vision of how things ought to be. In spite of his growing contempt for "reflection" and his increasing involvement with the world of political action, his writings have continued to serve as a means of escape from what he perceives as the grotesqueries of the real. The artist's penchant for writing away the anguish of reality is, of course, most obvious in the many fictional and dramatic renderings of his own emotional experience, *i.e.*, those recurring works wherein a LeRoi Jonesian figure (Ray, Clay, Walker, *et. al.*) serves an exorcistic function for his creator. It is in these projections that we see Baraka at his best. The artist himself, at one point, acknowledges the therapeutic value of these creations in yet another selection from *Tales*, "New-Sense":

> O world I want to change you, and these fantasies are sundays in the wet silence, gathering my strength about me, clear and free, for a hard thing. Which must be done, and gotten, in order that peace come, and be free, and unconditional.)

The "fantasies" are clearly the belletristic efforts that the man of action has come to scorn. In this attitude, we observe, of course, the extreme irony of the man hacking away at the ladder by which he rose.

Aside from an occasional horatory poem published in various "Third World" journals, Baraka's writing has been for the most part, limited to political tracts in behalf of the now-defunct Congress of African People (which became, under Baraka's influence, more and more conventionally Marxist-Leninist and less racially oriented) and more recently, the communist world-view in general. Examples of these later efforts are the long *African Congress: documentary of the first modern Pan-African Congress* (1972), edited and introduced by Baraka, "Toward Ideological Clarity," an article published in *Black World*, November, 1974, and *Poetry for the Advanced*, part of a retrospective collection of his verse published in 1979 by Morrow (*Selected Poetry of Amiri Baraka/LeRoi Jones*). Judging from the author's fervent involvement in the structuring of "a completely operational international political mechanism" and the relative dearth of even agit-prop art from his pen, Baraka has irrevocably cast his lot with what he calls the "expressive" forces. The literary works, personal projections as well as the blatantly propagandist efforts, are fragments of the old "soft loves" (see "I Substitute for the Dead Lecturer"). As such, the author attempts to devalue them, *i.e.*, to see them only as preparatory exercises. It is my hope that this study upholds the contradictory assertion that the works are worthy of study in and of themselves.

As we inspect the corpus of Baraka's writing, we are unavoidably aware of his faults—extreme privacy of reference, frequent experimental failure, and racist dogma, to name only a few. Nevertheless, we are also mindful of his merits—daring and frequently successful verbal approximations of jazz music, vibrant recreation of black speech, and a consummate portrayal of the black middle-class psyche. In spite of some obvious short-comings, Baraka, in the brief span of ten years, presented us with work of considerable promise. It is at least this writer's hope that the artist's increasingly myopic vision does not confirm the once-premature contention that "it is now necessary to inter him as a writer, young and kicking." However, at this point in his career, Baraka seems to be doing everything in his power to prove that grim prophecy sagacious.

Notes

[1]LeRoi Jones, *Home: Social Essays* (New York: William Morrow and Company, 1966), p. 9.

[2]*Home*, p. 10.

[3]*Ibid.*, p. 10.

[4]Harriet Beecher Stowe, *Uncle Tom's Cabin* (Cambridge: Cambridge University Press, 1899), p. 508.

[5]Larry G. Coleman, "LeRoi Jones' *Tales*: Sketches of the Artist as a Young Man Moving toward a Blacker Art," *Black Lines*, I, ii (Winter, 1970): 19.

[6]E. Franklin Frazier, *Black Bourgeoisie* (New York: Collier Press, 1968), p. 68.

7Ralph Ellison, *Invisible Man* (New York: New American Library (Signet), 1952), pp. 100-101.

8Coleman, p. 23.

9S. K. Oberbeck, "Black Daydreams, White Man's Nightmare," *Book World* (24 December 1967): 7.

Selected Bibliography of Works by Baraka

The Baptism and *The Toilet*. New York: Grove Press, 1966.

Black Magic Poetry. New York: Bobbs-Merrill Company, 1969.

Black Music. New York: William Morrow and Company, 1967.

Blues People: Negro Music in White America. New York: William Morrow and Company, 1963.

The Dead Lecturer. New York: Grove Press, 1964.

Dutchman and *The Slave*. New York: William Morrow and Company, 1964.

Four Black Revolutionary Plays. New York: Bobbs-Merrill Company, 1969.

Home: Social Essays. New York: William Morrow and Company, 1966.

With Fundi (Billy Abernathy) In Our Terribleness (Some Elements and Meaning in Black Style). New York: Bobbs-Merrill Company, 1970.

It's Nation Time Chicago: Third World Press, 1970.

Preface to a Twenty Volume Suicide Note. New York: Totem Press, 1961.

Raise Race Rays Raze: Essays since 1965. New York: Random House, 1971.

Selected Poetry of Amiri Baraka/LeRoi Jones: William Morrow and Company, 1979

Slave Ship: A Historical Pagaent. Newark: Jihad Production, 1969.

The System of Dante's Hell. New York: Grove Press, 1965.

Tales, New York: Grove Press, 1967.

* published under the name Amiri Baraka. All other published under the name LeRoi Jones

Index

To Raise, Destroy, and Create:

The Poetry, Drama, and Fiction of
Imamu Amiri Baraka
(LeRoi Jones)

Composed in IBM Electronic Selectric Composer *Journal Roman* and printed offset by McNaughton and Gunn, Incorporated, Ann Arbor, Michigan. The book was sewn and bound by Howard Dekker & Sons, Grand Rapids, Michigan. The paper on which the book is printed is the International Paper Company's *Bookmark*.

To Raise, Destroy, and Create is a Trenowyth book, the scholarly publishing division of The Whitston Publishing Company.

This edition consists in 500 casebound copies.